A MIDSUMMER NIGHT'S DREAM

William Shakespeare

Shakespeare and the Globe

Shakespeare was born in 1564, in Stratford, a small town in the Midlands. We know he was still in Stratford as an eighteen-year-old, when he got married. By 1592, he had moved to London, become an actor, and become a playwright. Shakespeare died in Stratford in 1616. He probably retired three or four years earlier, having bought land, and the biggest house in the town.

Shakespeare was successful. He became a shareholder in his acting company, and a shareholder in the Globe – the new theatre they built in 1599. His company was the best in the land, and the new king, James I, made them his company in 1603. They were known as the King's Men. Men, because women were not allowed to act on the stage. Boys or men played all the women's parts. Shakespeare wrote at least 40 plays, of which only 38 survive. Only eighteen of his plays were printed in his lifetime, including *A Midsummer Night's Dream*. After his death, his colleagues published a collection of 36 of his plays, known as the *First Folio*.

London Theatres

There were professional companies of actors working in London from the middle of the sixteenth century. They usually performed in inns, and the city council often tried to ban them. The solution was to have their own purpose-built theatre, just outside the area the council controlled. The first, simply called *The Theatre*, opened in 1576.

Shakespeare's Globe today

Sam Wanamaker, an American actor and director, founded the Shakespeare's Globe Trust in 1970. Sam could not understand why there wasn't a proper memorial to the world's greatest playwright in the city where he had lived and worked. He started fundraising to build a new Globe Theatre. Sadly, Sam died before the theatre opened in 1997.

Heavens

Upper stage

Stage

Galleries

Entrances

Yard

The new Globe is the third. The first burnt down in 1613 during a performance of Shakespeare's Henry VIII. The King's Men rebuilt it on the same site, and it re-opened in 1614. This second one was closed in 1642, and pulled down in 1647 to build houses.

The new Globe is 200 yards from the original site, and is based on all the evidence that survives. It has been built using the same materials as the original, and using the same building techniques.

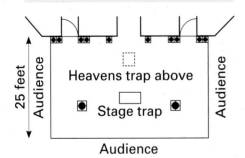

The stage trap opened into the area under the stage. The heavens trap was not on the stage, but above it. Actors playing gods might be lowered down to the stage through it.

The first Globe Theatre

The Globe Theatre was open-air. If it rained, some of the audience got wet. There was no special lighting; so the plays were performed in the afternoon, in daylight. This meant that, unlike most modern theatres, the actors could see the audience, as well as the audience see the actors (and each other). It may have held as many as 3,000 people, with, perhaps, 1,000 standing in the yard. They paid one old penny (there were 240 in £1). The rest sat in the three galleries, so they were under cover if it rained. They paid more, at least two pence, and as much as six pence for the best seats. The audience was a mixture of social classes, with the poorer people standing.

The stage was large, and extended into the middle of the yard, so there were people on three sides. We think it had three entrances in the back wall – a door on either side, and a larger one in the middle. There was a roof so the actors, and their expensive costumes, would always be in the dry. The underside of this roof, called *the heavens*, was painted with the signs of the zodiac. There was also an upper stage, which was sometimes used in plays, sometimes used by the musicians, and also had the most expensive seats in the theatre. All the rest of the audience could see people who sat in the upper stage area. If you sat there, people could see who you were, that you could afford to sit there, and your expensive clothes.

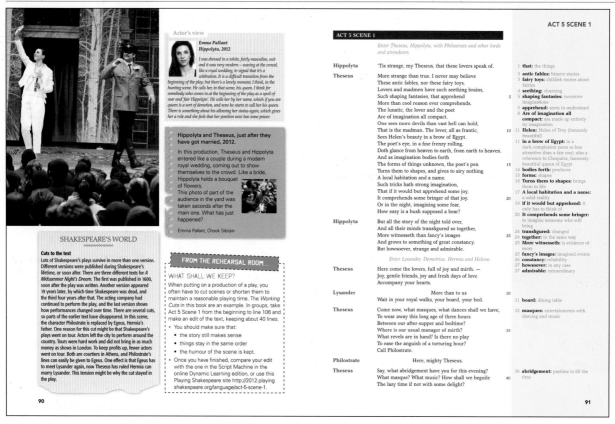

The **play text** is the place to start. What characters say is in black, and stage directions are in blue. Line numbers, on the right, help you refer to an exact place.

	In least, speak most to my capacity.	105
	[Enter Philostrate.]	
Philostrate	So please your grace, the Prologue is addressed.	
Theseus	Let him approach.	
	Trumpets sound offstage.	
	Enter Quince as the Prologue.	
Prologue (Quince)	*If we offend, it is with our good will.*	
	That you should think, we come not to offend,	
	But with good will. To show our simple skill,	110

Some stage directions, like the first one above, have square brackets. This means they are not in the original text, but have been added to help you when you read. They tell you what you would see on the stage.

> 203–4 **walls are so wilful …**
> **warning:** playing with the
> proverb 'walls have ears'

The **glossary** is right next to the text. To help you find the word or phrase you want, each entry has the line number in blue, then the word or phrase in black, and finally the explanation in blue again. To keep it clear, sometimes, as in this case, some words from the original have been missed out, and replaced with three dots.

Actor's view boxes are exactly what they say. Actors who have played the part at the Globe tell you what they thought about their character and some of the choices they made.

Green boxes go with the photos. They tell you what you are looking at, and give you a question to think about. Unless the question says otherwise, the answer will be in the play text on the opposite page. The names of the actors are in smaller print.

From the rehearsal room gives you the exercises actors use during rehearsals to help them understand the play. They come with questions that help you reflect on what you can learn from the exercise.

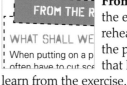

Working Cuts sometimes go with the *From the rehearsal room* activities. They cut lines from the scene so you can do the activity in the time you have available.

Shakespeare's World boxes give you important context for the play. For example, this box explains why there are different versions of the text. Understanding context like this will improve your understanding of the play.

Finally, **Director's Note** boxes come at the end of every scene. They give you a quick summary of the most important things in the scene, and a focus to think about.

The Characters in the play

This book uses photographs from three productions of *A Midsummer Night's Dream* at Shakespeare's Globe. The actors and creative teams of each production are an important part of the book.

	2002 Director: *Mike Alfreds*	2008 Director: *Jonathan Munby*	2012 Director: *Bill Buckhurst*
The Athenians Courtiers			
Theseus, Duke of Athens	Paul Higgins	Tom Mannion	Chook Sibtain
Hippolyta, Queen of the Amazons	Geraldine Alexander	Siobhan Redmond	Emma Pallant
Lysander, a young courtier	Richard Katz	Christopher Brandon	Peter Bray
Demetrius, a young courtier	Keith Dunphy	Oliver Boot	Richard James-Neale
Hermia, in love with Lysander	Philippa Stanton	Pippa Nixon	Louise Collins
Helena, in love with Demetrius	Louise Bush	Laura Rogers	Carlyss Peer
Egeus, Hermia's father	Gary Lilburn	Richard Clews	William Oxborrow
Philostrate, Master of the Revels	Simon Trinder	Michael Jibson	Fergal McElherron
The Mechanicals (workmen)			
Peter Quince, a carpenter	Paul Trussell	Michael Matus	William Oxborrow
Nick Bottom, a weaver	John Ramm	Paul Hunter	Russell Layton
Francis Flute, a bellows-mender	Aled Pugh	Peter Bankolé	Peter Bray
Tom Snout, a tinker	Patrick Lennox	Jonathan Bond	Richard James-Neale
Snug, a joiner	Jem Wall	Robert Goodale	Louise Collins
Robin Starveling, a tailor	Ryan Early	Sam Parks	Carlyss Peer
The Fairies			
Oberon, King of the Fairies	Paul Higgins	Tom Mannion	Chook Sibtain
Titania, Queen of the Fairies	Geraldine Alexander	Siobhan Redmond	Emma Pallant
Puck, or Robin Goodfellow	Simon Trinder	Michael Jibson	Fergal McElherron
A Fairy, who serves Titania	Ryan Early	Adam Burton	Carlyss Peer
Peaseblossom, who serves Titania		Bethan Walker	Peter Bray
Cobweb, who serves Titania		Richard Clews	Louise Collins
Moth, who serves Titania		Siân Williams	William Oxborrow
Mustardseed, who serves Titania		Adam Burton	Richard James-Neale
		Peter Bankolé	
Lords and attendants in Athens, other Fairies who attend Oberon and Titania			
Designer	Jenny Tiramani	Mike Britton	Isla Shaw
Composer	Claire van Kampen	Olly Fox	Olly Fox
Choreographer		Siân Williams	Siân Williams
Musical Director	Sarah Homer		Steve Bentley-Klein

PUNCTUATION

- Together as a group, read Egeus' speech in lines 22–45 out loud.
- Tap your desk lightly whenever you encounter any punctuation mark (including dashes).
- Now read the speech again. This time only tap the desk when you come to a full stop.
- What difference does this make?

1 What is Egeus' emotional state? Quote from the text to support your answer.

2 How would you describe him in this scene? Give three characteristics.

3 What does Egeus want Duke Theseus to do?

4 What does he think of Lysander? Quote from the text to support your answer.

5 Do we find out any reason for him wanting Demetrius, rather than Lysander, to marry his daughter?

SHAKESPEARE'S WORLD

Hippolyta and Theseus

In this scene, Shakespeare introduces us to the Duke and his bride. Shakespeare's audience would have been familiar with the ancient story of Theseus and Hippolyta. Hippolyta was Queen of the Amazons, a race of warrior women. Theseus was King of Athens.

In William Painter's *Novel of the Amazons,* which we know Shakespeare used as a source, he says that the Amazons 'were most excellent warriors', but that they 'murdered certain of their husbands'. There is more than one version of the story of Theseus and Hippolyta. But most Elizabethans knew that Theseus had lured Hippolyta to his ship, kidnapped her, and carried her away to Athens. Some versions of the story say Theseus raped her and forced her to marry him. The kidnapping of Hippolyta is said to have sparked the great battle between the Amazons and the Athenians, the ultimate battle between the sexes. As the queen of a country ruled by women, Hippolyta may be surprised at the lack of power and status women have in Athens.

Hippolyta, with Theseus in the background, 2012.

This photo was taken before anybody speaks. Hippolyta was on stage first, and then she was joined by Theseus.
Read the *Shakespeare's World* box, and think about what these two lines mean – Theseus says them (lines 16–17).
'Hippolyta, I woo'd thee with my sword, And won thy love doing thee injuries.'

1 Look carefully at Hippolyta. How have the director and designer helped the audience understand what has happened before the play starts? Explain your answer.

2 Look carefully at Theseus. Again, how have the director and designer helped the audience understand what has happened before the play starts? Explain your answer.

Chook Sibtain, Emma Pallant

Enter Theseus, Hippolyta, Philostrate, and others.

Theseus	Now, fair Hippolyta, our nuptial hour
	Draws on apace. Four happy days bring in
	Another moon. But O, methinks, how slow
	This old moon wanes! She lingers my desires
	Like to a step-dame, or a dowager, 5
	Long withering out a young man's revenue.

Hippolyta	Four days will quickly steep themselves in night,
	Four nights will quickly dream away the time,
	And then the moon, like to a silver bow
	New-bent in heaven, shall behold the night 10
	Of our solemnities.

Theseus	Go Philostrate,
	Stir up the Athenian youth to merriments,
	Awake the pert and nimble spirit of mirth,
	Turn melancholy forth to funerals.
	The pale companion is not for our pomp. 15

[Exit Philostrate.]

	Hippolyta, I woo'd thee with my sword,
	And won thy love doing thee injuries.
	But I will wed thee in another key,
	With pomp, with triumph, and with revelling.

Enter Egeus, his daughter Hermia, Lysander, and Demetrius.

Egeus	Happy be Theseus, our renowned Duke. 20

Theseus	Thanks good Egeus. What's the news with thee?

Egeus	Full of vexation come I, with complaint
	Against my child, my daughter Hermia. —
	Stand forth, Demetrius. — My noble lord,
	This man hath my consent to marry her. — 25
	Stand forth, Lysander. — And my gracious Duke,
	This man hath bewitch'd the bosom of my child.
	Thou, thou, Lysander, thou hast given her rhymes,
	And interchanged love-tokens with my child.
	Thou hast by moonlight at her window sung 30
	With feigning voice verses of feigning love.
	And stol'n the impression of her fantasy
	With bracelets of thy hair, rings, gauds, conceits,
	Knacks, trifles, nosegays, sweetmeats (messengers
	Of strong prevailment in unharden'd youth). 35
	With cunning hast thou filched my daughter's heart,
	Turned her obedience (which is due to me)
	To stubborn harshness. And, my gracious Duke,
	Be it so she will not here, before your Grace,
	Consent to marry with Demetrius, 40
	I beg the ancient privilege of Athens.
	As she is mine, I may dispose of her,
	Which shall be either to this gentleman,

1-2 **our nuptial hour Draws on apace:** it will soon be our wedding day

2-3 **Four happy days ... Another moon:** only four days until the new moon

4 **wanes:** wears itself out

4 **lingers my desires:** makes the waiting seem impossibly long

5 **step-dame:** stepmother

5 **dowager:** widow

6 **Long withering out ... revenue:** taking a long time to die, so spending the inheritance

7 **steep themselves in:** dissolve into

9 **silver bow:** reference to the shape of the new moon, which is a thin bright crescent. It may also be a reference to Diana, Roman goddess of hunting, the moon and chastity

11 **solemnities:** wedding ceremonies

13 **pert:** quick-witted

15 **The pale companion:** sadness

15 **pomp:** celebration

16-7 **I woo'd thee ... doing thee injuries:** I captured you

19 **triumph:** public celebrations

22 **vexation:** anger

27 **bewitch'd the bosom of my child:** charmed her heart away

31 **feigning:** twice in the line for a double meaning: 1) soft; 2) deceitful

32 **stol'n the impression of her fantasy:** made her think of nothing but him

33-4 **gauds, conceits ... sweetmeats:** cheap, flashy presents

34-5 **(messengers ... unharden'd youth):** seductive to a silly young girl

36 **filched:** stolen

39 **Be it so:** if

41 **ancient privilege:** traditional legal right

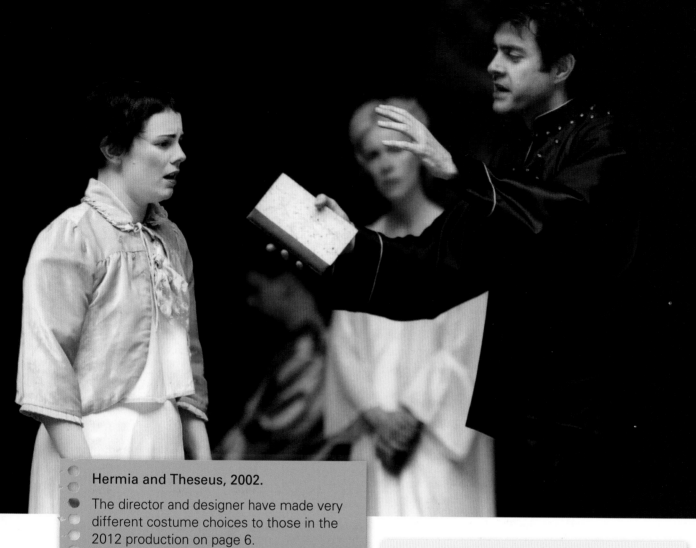

Hermia and Theseus, 2002.

The director and designer have made very different costume choices to those in the 2012 production on page 6.

1 What do these costumes suggest, and how might that fit the world of this play?

2 Another character is standing behind them, watching what is going on. Who might this be? Give reasons for your answer.

Philippa Stanton, Paul Higgins

Actor's view

Siobhan Redmond
Hippolyta and Titania, 2008

In the most unlikely of situations, two middle-aged people have actually fallen in love. And then this other extraordinary thing happens, which gives Hippolyta something of a reality check. I think that a woman who is a monarch in her own right would find it extraordinary that women are treated as disposable items. It will give her pause for thought [about] the man who she has fallen in love with. I withdraw from him a little as the scene develops; it seems to me to be the most logical way through it. So, essentially, she is in a huff, off stage, until we see her in a huff on stage, in Act 4 Scene 1. As usual, the lines don't help much, because Hippolyta doesn't speak much.

SHAKESPEARE'S WORLD

Arranged marriages

In Elizabethan England, fathers normally chose their daughter's husband. Age and social status were the main reasons for their choice. The groom and the bride's father would discuss the terms of a marriage. Usually, a father paid a dowry to the groom to help support his daughter's living costs.

In the play, these families are rich and powerful, and the right marriage would help both families.

Egeus had decided Demetrius would be Hermia's husband. This means Lysander wooed Hermia without her father's consent, and most of the original audience would think he behaved badly. They would understand Egeus' complaint that Hermia must marry the man he chooses for her. This was the normal custom. Most of the audience would think Hermia disobeying her father by wanting to marry Lysander was wrong. Theseus agrees that Hermia must obey her father.

However, by Elizabethan standards, Egeus' behaviour is rash and cruel towards his daughter. And Theseus' threat against her life if she disobeys her father goes far beyond what would have seemed reasonable in Shakespeare's day.

	Or to her death, according to our law	
	Immediately provided in that case.	45

Theseus
What say you, Hermia? Be advised fair maid.
To you your father should be as a god.
One that composed your beauties, yea and one
To whom you are but as a form in wax
By him imprinted, and within his power   50
To leave the figure or disfigure it.
Demetrius is a worthy gentleman.

Hermia
So is Lysander.

Theseus
                    In himself he is.
But in this kind, wanting your father's voice,
The other must be held the worthier.   55

Hermia
I would my father looked but with my eyes.

Theseus
Rather your eyes must with his judgment look.

Hermia
I do entreat your grace to pardon me.
I know not by what power I am made bold,
Nor how it may concern my modesty,   60
In such a presence, here to plead my thoughts.
But I beseech your Grace that I may know
The worst that may befall me in this case,
If I refuse to wed Demetrius.

Theseus
Either to die the death, or to abjure   65
For ever the society of men.
Therefore, fair Hermia, question your desires,
Know of your youth, examine well your blood,
Whether (if you yield not to your father's choice)
You can endure the livery of a nun.   70
For aye to be in shady cloister mewed,
To live a barren sister all your life,
Chanting faint hymns to the cold fruitless moon.
Thrice-blessed they that master so their blood,
To undergo such maiden pilgrimage,   75
But earthlier happy is the rose distilled,
Than that which withering on the virgin thorn,
Grows, lives, and dies, in single blessedness.

Hermia
So will I grow, so live, so die, my lord,
Ere I will yield my virgin patent up   80
Unto his lordship, whose unwishèd yoke
My soul consents not to give sovereignty.

Theseus
Take time to pause, and, by the next new moon,
(The sealing-day betwixt my love and me
For everlasting bond of fellowship)   85
Upon that day either prepare to die
For disobedience to your father's will,
Or else to wed Demetrius, as he would,
Or on Diana's altar to protest
For aye, austerity and single life.   90

---

45 **Immediately provided in that case:** written to deal with just this situation
46 **Be advised:** take my advice
48 **composed your beauties:** made you as you are
49–50 **but as a form in wax By him imprinted:** nothing but a wax figure he's made
54 **in this kind:** in these circumstances
54 **wanting:** without
54 **voice:** support
56 **I would:** I wish
57 **Rather:** instead
58 **I do entreat:** I beg
60 **how it may concern my modesty:** whether I will seem to be too pushy
63 **befall me:** happen to me
65–6 **abjure For ever the society of men:** become a nun
68 **Know of your youth:** consider how young you are
68 **your blood:** your feelings, passions
69 **yield not to:** don't accept
70 **livery:** uniform
71 **For aye to be … cloister mewed:** to be shut up in a gloomy convent forever
72 **barren sister:** childless nun
73 **fruitless:** childless
74 **master so:** can so control
75 **maiden pilgrimage:** the life of a virgin nun
76–8 **But earthlier happy … single blessedness:** women who are married (and have children) have a happier life than nuns but nuns will be happier in heaven
80 **Ere I will yield my virgin patent up:** before I give up my virginity
81–2 **whose unwishèd yoke … sovereignty:** who I don't want to marry, and therefore obey
83 **pause:** think it over
84 **sealing-day:** wedding day
84 **betwixt:** between
88 **as he would:** as your father wants you to
89–90 **on Diana's altar … single life:** to enter a nunnery forever

9

Lysander and Hermia, 2012.

Which lines do you think were being spoken as this photo was taken? Give reasons for your answer.

Peter Bray, Louise Collins

FROM THE REHEARSAL ROOM...

WHO LOVES WHO?

- In groups of six read from line 91 to 112. Decide who will play the four speaking parts, with two playing the non-speaking parts of Helena and Hermia.

- Stand in two rows of three, so each person faces another person.

- Read through the scene and each time your character says a pronoun or a proper name, point at who or what you are talking to or about. Point in an exaggerated manner, particularly when talking about Helena or Hermia.

Copy the diagram below, and draw arrows to show your answer.

a) Before the play began, who loved who?

b) Now, at the beginning of the play, who loves who?

Before the play		At the start of the play (1.1)	
Hermia	Helena	Hermia	Helena
Lysander	Demetrius	Lysander	Demetrius

FROM THE REHEARSAL ROOM...

IN MY WORLD

Hippolyta remains silent during most of Act 1 Scene 1. Theseus' line *Come my Hippolyta, what cheer, my love?* (line 122) suggests she may be unhappy.

- Read the information from the *Shakespeare's World* box on page 6 about Hippolyta and the Amazons.

- Then, in pairs, read the whole scene from Egeus' entrance (line 20) to his exit (line 127). Note each thing that is said or happens which might upset Hippolyta.

- Discuss how Hippolyta might react to each thing. You might start each reaction with 'In my world …' (For instance: 'In my world fathers don't own their daughters'.)

1 How different is Hippolyta's world from that of Athens?

2 What challenges might Hippolyta encounter in her new life with Theseus?

3 As Hippolyta, write a new marriage law for Athens.

Demetrius Relent, sweet Hermia, and Lysander, yield
Thy crazèd title to my certain right.

Lysander You have her father's love, Demetrius,
Let me have Hermia's. Do you marry him.

Egeus Scornful Lysander! True, he hath my love,
And what is mine, my love shall render him.
And she is mine, and all my right of her
I do estate unto Demetrius.

Lysander I am, my lord, as well derived as he,
As well possessed. My love is more than his.
My fortunes every way as fairly ranked
(If not with vantage) as Demetrius'.
And, which is more than all these boasts can be,
I am beloved of beauteous Hermia.
Why should not I then prosecute my right?
Demetrius, I'll avouch it to his head,
Made love to Nedar's daughter, Helena,
And won her soul. And she, sweet lady, dotes,
Devoutly dotes, dotes in idolatry,
Upon this spotted and inconstant man.

Theseus I must confess that I have heard so much,
And with Demetrius thought to have spoke thereof.
But being over-full of self-affairs,
My mind did lose it. But Demetrius come,
And come Egeus, you shall go with me,
I have some private schooling for you both.
For you, fair Hermia, look you arm yourself
To fit your fancies to your father's will,
Or else the law of Athens yields you up
(Which by no means we may extenuate)
To death, or to a vow of single life.
Come my Hippolyta, what cheer, my love?
Demetrius and Egeus go along,
I must employ you in some business
Against our nuptial, and confer with you
Of something nearly that concerns yourselves.

Egeus With duty and desire we follow you.

They all exit, except Lysander and Hermia.

Lysander How now, my love? Why is your cheek so pale?
How chance the roses there do fade so fast?

Hermia Belike for want of rain, which I could well
Beteem them from the tempest of my eyes.

Lysander Ay me! For aught that I could ever read,
Could ever hear by tale or history,
The course of true love never did run smooth,
But either it was different in blood —

Hermia O cross! Too high to be enthralled to low.

Lysander Or else misgraffèd in respect of years —

95

100

105

110

115

120

125

130

135

92 crazèd title: flawed demand

94 Do you: why don't you?

96 render: give to

98 estate unto: legally transfer to
99 as well derived: from as good a family
100 As well possessed: as rich
101 My fortunes … fairly ranked: I will inherit just as much
102 with vantage: more than
105 prosecute my right: press you to accept my request to marry Hermia
106 avouch it to his head: say it to his face
107 Made love to: courted
108 dotes: loves madly
109 dotes in idolatry: worships as a god
110 spotted: immoral
112 thereof: about it
113 over-full of self-affairs: caught up in my own business

114 My mind did lose it: I forgot
116 private schooling: advice to give in private
117 look you arm yourself: prepare yourself
118 fit your fancies: shape your wishes
120 by no means we may extenuate: I can't change
122 what cheer: what's the matter?

125 Against our nuptial: to do with the wedding
126 nearly that: that closely

130 Belike: probably
131 Beteem: flood
131 tempest of my eyes: tears
132 For aught: from anything
135 it was different in blood: the lovers were from different social classes
136 O cross!: what a burden!
136 Too high … to low: too important to be married to someone of lower birth
137 misgraffèd in respect of years: the age difference was too great

11

Hermia and Lysander, 2008.

This photo was taken about line 131. Compare it with the photo on page 10, taken about the same point. What are the similarities and differences between the two productions at this point?

Pippa Nixon, Christopher Brandon

FROM THE REHEARSAL ROOM...

WHAT WOULD I DO?

After you have read the play up to line 155, in groups think about Hermia and Lysander's problem.

- Discuss what you would want to do if you found yourself in this predicament.
- Would your solution work for a young couple when Shakespeare was writing? (It will help to look back at the *Shakespeare's World* box on page 8.)
- Make a freeze frame to show what you think Hermia and Lysander are feeling.
- Show the image to the rest of the class and let them comment on what they see.

1 Do you think the way a modern audience thinks about Hermia and Lysander's problem will be different to the way Shakespeare's original audience thought about it? Explain your answer.

Actor's view

Louise Collins
Hermia, 2012

I think it is really important at the beginning of the play that she is very young, in a school uniform, but has this massive emotion, love, which makes her quite mature. So she's got two things going on, her youth, and this big feeling. Out of that comes this plan to run away. And then Helena comes in, weeping, feeling full of self-pity. I think that Hermia feels an enormous amount of guilt for the fact that Demetrius is in love with her, and not with Helena. We have rhyming couplets, which is interesting, so we are very connected and we have a great friendship, but at the same time, there is nothing I can do to help. I think in [telling] the secret to Helena – that we are going to run away – that is me trying to comfort her and say look, we're going to go so maybe all will be well with Demetrius. And that is when everything goes wrong.

Hermia	O spite! Too old to be engaged to young.
Lysander	Or else it stood upon the choice of friends —
Hermia	O hell! To choose love by another's eyes.
Lysander	Or, if there were a sympathy in choice,
	War, death, or sickness did lay siege to it,
	Making it momentary as a sound,
	Swift as a shadow, short as any dream,
	Brief as the lightning in the collied night,
	That, in a spleen, unfolds both heav'n and earth,
	And ere a man hath power to say "Behold!"
	The jaws of darkness do devour it up.
	So quick bright things come to confusion.
Hermia	If then true lovers have been ever crossed,
	It stands as an edict in destiny.
	Then let us teach our trial patience,
	Because it is a customary cross,
	As due to love as thoughts and dreams and sighs,
	Wishes and tears, poor Fancy's followers.
Lysander	A good persuasion. Therefore hear me, Hermia,
	I have a widow aunt, a dowager
	Of great revenue, and she hath no child.
	From Athens is her house remote se'en leagues,
	And she respects me as her only son.
	There, gentle Hermia, may I marry thee,
	And to that place the sharp Athenian law
	Cannot pursue us. If thou lov'st me, then
	Steal forth thy father's house tomorrow night,
	And in the wood, a league without the town,
	(Where I did meet thee once with Helena
	To do observance to a morn of May)
	There will I stay for thee.
Hermia	My good Lysander,
	I swear to thee by Cupid's strongest bow,
	By his best arrow with the golden head,
	By the simplicity of Venus' doves,
	By that which knitteth souls and prospers loves,
	And by that fire which burned the Carthage queen
	When the false Troyan under sail was seen,
	By all the vows that ever men have broke,
	(In number more than ever women spoke),
	In that same place thou hast appointed me,
	Tomorrow truly will I meet with thee.
Lysander	Keep promise, love. Look, here comes Helena.
	Enter Helena.
Hermia	God speed fair Helena. Whither away?
Helena	Call you me fair? That fair again unsay.
	Demetrius loves your fair. O happy fair!
	Your eyes are lode-stars, and your tongue's sweet air

139 **stood upon:** depended on
139 **friends:** relatives

141 **if there were a sympathy in choice:** if the lovers could choose each other

145 **collied:** coal-black
146 **a spleen:** a flash of temper
146 **unfolds:** lights up
147 **ere:** before
149 **So quick ... come to confusion:** life is brought to ruin as quickly as this
151 **It stands as an edict in destiny:** it's our fate
152 **teach our trial patience:** put up with it
153 **a customary cross:** the normal fate of lovers
154 **As due to:** as much a part of
155 **Fancy's:** love's (seen as a person)
157–8 **a dowager Of great revenue:** a rich widow
159 **remote se'en leagues:** seven leagues (21 miles) away
160 **respects:** looks on

164 **Steal forth:** creep out of
165 **a league:** about 3 miles

167 **To do observance:** to celebrate
167 **a morn of May:** May Day
168 **stay:** wait
169 **Cupid:** the god of love (son of Venus, the goddess of love) whose golden-headed arrows made people fall in love (often shown blindfolded)
173 **the Carthage queen:** Dido, Queen of Carthage; said to have killed herself on a funeral bonfire when her lover, Aeneas, left her
174 **the false Troyan:** Aeneas

180 **God speed:** God go with you (a greeting)
180 **fair:** lovely
180 **Whither away?:** where are you off to?
181 **unsay:** take back
183 **lode-stars:** guiding stars
183 **your tongue's sweet air:** your voice

Line numbers: 140, 145, 150, 155, 160, 165, 170, 175, 180

A

B

C

A Hermia, Helena, and Lysander, 2008. Helena has got trapped between them, just as Hermia and Lysander kiss goodbye (lines 224–5).

Pippa Nixon, Laura Rogers, Christopher Brandon

B Hermia and Helena, 2012. 'And good luck grant thee thy Demetrius.' (line 221)

Louise Collins, Carlyss Peer

C Helena and Hermia, 2002. 'And in the wood, where often you and I/Upon faint primrose-beds were wont to lie' (lines 214–5).

Louise Bush, Philippa Stanton

1 Describe the costume choices that were made in each of the three productions.

2 Which do you think works best? Give reasons for your answer.

3 Look at the body language of the actors in each photograph. Which do you think best captures the situation between Hermia and Helena? Quote from the text to support your answer.

More tuneable than lark to shepherd's ear.
When wheat is green, when hawthorn buds appear.   185
Sickness is catching. O were favour so,
Yours would I catch, fair Hermia, ere I go
My ear should catch your voice, my eye your eye,
My tongue should catch your tongue's sweet melody.
Were the world mine, Demetrius being bated,   190
The rest I'd give to be to you translated.
O, teach me how you look, and with what art
You sway the motion of Demetrius' heart.

Hermia I frown upon him, yet he loves me still.

Helena O that your frowns would teach my smiles such skill.   195

Hermia I give him curses, yet he gives me love.

Helena O that my prayers could such affection move.

Hermia The more I hate, the more he follows me.

Helena The more I love, the more he hateth me.

Hermia His folly, Helena, is none of mine.   200

Helena None but your beauty. Would that fault were mine.

Hermia Take comfort. He no more shall see my face,
Lysander and myself will fly this place.
Before the time I did Lysander see,
Seemed Athens as a paradise to me.   205
O then, what graces in my love do dwell,
That he hath turned a heav'n unto a hell!

Lysander Helen, to you our minds we will unfold.
Tomorrow night, when Phoebe doth behold
Her silver visage in the watery glass,   210
Decking with liquid pearl the bladed grass
(A time that lovers' flights doth still conceal)
Through Athens' gates have we devised to steal.

Hermia And in the wood, where often you and I
Upon faint primrose-beds were wont to lie,   215
Emptying our bosoms of their counsel swelled,
There my Lysander and myself shall meet,
And thence from Athens turn away our eyes
To seek new friends and strange companions.
Farewell sweet playfellow, pray thou for us,   220
And good luck grant thee thy Demetrius.
Keep word Lysander, we must starve our sight
From lovers' food till morrow deep midnight.

Lysander I will my Hermia.   *Exit Hermia.*
          Helena, adieu.
As you on him, Demetrius dote on you!   225

                              Exit Lysander.

---

184 **tuneable:** tuneful, pleasant sounding

186 **favour:** a person's beauty and manners

190 **Demetrius being bated:** double meaning: 1) except for Demetrius; 2) Demetrius being caught
191 **translated:** changed how you like
192 **art:** skill
193 **sway the motion:** affect the direction of

200 **folly:** foolish behaviour
200 **none of mine:** not my fault

203 **will fly this place:** are going to run away from Athens

209 **Phoebe:** another name for the goddess of the moon
210 **visage:** face
210 **watery glass:** mirror-like water
211 **Decking:** decorating
211 **liquid pearl:** dew
212 **still:** always
213 **devised to steal:** planned to slip away
215 **were wont to lie:** often lay
216 **Emptying our bosoms ... counsel swelled:** telling each other everything
218 **thence:** from there
219 **strange:** as yet unknown

222 **Keep word:** don't break your promise

Helena, 2008.

Which line do you think Helena is saying when this photo was taken?

a) 'He will not know what all but he do know'

b) 'Through Athens I am thought as fair as she.'

Give reasons for your answer.

Laura Rogers

Helena

How happy some o'er other some can be!
Through Athens I am thought as fair as she.
But what of that? Demetrius thinks not so.
He will not know what all but he do know,
And as he errs, doting on Hermia's eyes,
So I, admiring of his qualities.
Things base and vile, holding no quantity,
Love can transpose to form and dignity.
Love looks not with the eyes, but with the mind,
And therefore is wing'd Cupid painted blind.
Nor hath Love's mind of any judgement taste,
Wings, and no eyes, figure unheedy haste.
And therefore is Love said to be a child,
Because in choice he is so oft beguiled.
As waggish boys, in game, themselves forswear,
So the boy Love is perjured every where.
For, ere Demetrius looked on Hermia's eyne,
He hailed down oaths that he was only mine,
And when this hail some heat from Hermia felt,
So he dissolved, and showers of oaths did melt.
I will go tell him of fair Hermia's flight.
Then to the wood will he tomorrow night
Pursue her; and for this intelligence,
If I have thanks, it is a dear expense.
But herein mean I to enrich my pain,
To have his sight thither, and back again.

Exit Helena.

226 **How happy some ... can be!:** some people are given more happiness than others
230 **errs:** goes astray
231 **So I:** I also go astray
232 **base:** of poor quality
232 **vile:** revolting
232 **holding:** having
233 **transpose:** make seem
233 **form:** sensible proportion
236 **Nor hath Love's mind ... taste:** love doesn't choose sensibly
237 **figure:** show
237 **unheedy:** careless
239 **beguiled:** deceived, led astray
240 **waggish:** mischievous
240 **themselves forswear:** break their word
241 **is perjured:** breaks his word
242 **eyne:** eyes
248 **intelligence:** information
249 **it is a dear expense:** I'll pay a high price for it (because he'll chase Hermia)
250 **herein:** here's how
250 **mean I:** I intend
250 **enrich:** make even greater
251 **To have his sight:** to be able to look on him
251 **thither:** there

FROM THE REHEARSAL ROOM...

WHO LOVED WHO?

- Read Helena's speech in lines 226–251.
- According to Helena who loved who, and who loves who now?
1 Copy the diagram below, and draw arrows to show your answer. You may need to use two colours to show 'before' and 'now'.

According to Helena (1.1)

Hermia	Helena

Lysander	Demetrius

Director's Note, 1.1

✔ Theseus has defeated Hippolyta in a war, and will marry her in four days' time.
✔ Egeus is determined his daughter, Hermia, will marry Demetrius, but she loves Lysander.
✔ Theseus rules Hermia must obey her father, become a nun, or die.
✔ Hermia and Lysander plan to run away from Athens, so they can marry. They tell Helena (who loves Demetrius). She decides to tell Demetrius.
✔ Is Helena's plan to tell Demetrius a good one?

EXAMINER'S NOTES, 1.1

These questions help you to explore many aspects of *A Midsummer Night's Dream*. Support each answer by reference to the text. At GCSE, your teacher will tell you which aspects are relevant to how your Shakespeare response will be assessed.

❶ Character and plot development

Act 1 Scene 1 establishes the main romantic plot of the play. This focuses on complications between the lovers Hermia, Lysander, Helena and Demetrius. Hermia faces death or life as a nun if she refuses to marry Demetrius, her father's choice for her husband. Shakespeare uses a situation that could be a basis of tragedy. However, he presents the complications, mistakes and confusions that follow from Hermia's choice to run away with Lysander as a matter of comedy.

1   In what ways does Act 1 Scene 1 introduce the basis of a plot to be developed in the next few Acts?
2   How far could the events of Act 1 Scene 1 be used as the introduction to a tragedy?
3   How does Shakespeare create a sense of Hermia's independence and defiance in lines 53–82?
4   What do you think Shakespeare does to make the audience sympathise with Helena before she is on stage in lines 105–116, in her envy of Demetrius' love for Hermia in lines 180–207 and in her plan to win Demetrius back in lines 226–251?
5   Which of Egeus' words conveys his sense of injury (lines 22–45)?

❷ Characterisation and voice: dramatic language

Shakespeare creates believable characters by giving them speeches that are rich in words that express feelings and attitudes, as well as status.

6   Which words in Egeus' opening speech (lines 27–38) convey his attitude to Lysander and his feelings about Hermia's love for him?
7   Which words in Theseus' speech (lines 65–78) emphasise the unpleasantness of the life that Hermia will have to accept if she refuses to obey her father?

❸ Themes and ideas

Although the play is a comedy to entertain, it involves ideas that relate to people's everyday lives. For example, that lovers can be jealous, that love can cause disruptions in the family, that love can be unrequited and that, most of all, the course of true love never did run smooth.

8   Shakespeare begins the play with Theseus' happy announcement of his marriage celebrations. Is there anything to suggest that his relationship with Hippolyta may not always have 'run smooth' (lines 1–19)?
9   How does Shakespeare create a contrasting sense of love leading to bitterness and conflict in lines 22–45?
10 In what ways does Shakespeare use Egeus and Helena to present different ideas about love in lines 30–35 and 232–251?
11 Egeus is so angry at his daughter's refusal to obey him that he threatens the law of Athens to punish her with death if she will not marry Demetrius (lines 42–45). How does Shakespeare use Theseus's speech in lines 65–78 to emphasise Egeus' harshness, and Theseus' speech in lines 111–12 to suggest that Egeus may not be judging the two young men equally?

EXAMINER'S TIP

Voice

Voice is the kind of speech behaviour that is so typical of a character that an audience can recognise who is speaking from a small extract. This may be because of accent, dialect or a personal language habit.

A character may speak in many different ways according to who they are speaking to, and how they feel. A character's language may show signs of attitude or of feeling, so that an audience can tell if the character is worried, angry, curious, challenging or trying to persuade.

For example, Egeus is a respectable gentleman in Athens who speaks with courtesy to the Duke; e.g. 'My noble lord', 'my gracious Duke' and 'your Grace' (lines 24, 26, 39).

His personal feelings of injury, however, are conveyed by his repeated use of the possessive 'my', in 'my child', 'my daughter', 'as she is mine' (lines 22, 27, 29, 36, 42).

His attitude to Lysander is conveyed by his use of negative words such as 'bewitch'd', 'feigning', 'cunning' and 'filched' (lines 27, 31, 36).

EXAMINER'S NOTES, 1.1

4 Performance

The way Egeus (and others) are presented in this opening scene can affect the way an audience sees him. He could be played as an old, cantankerous man, or as a smart-suited younger man who doesn't trust Lysander dressed as a hippy. His relationship with Demetrius could be conveyed by having Demetrius dressed similarly to Egeus, standing at his side, holding a briefcase from which Egeus pulls out bracelets, rings, nosegays and 'gauds', thrown with contempt to the floor.

12 How would you advise Lysander, Demetrius and Egeus to perform lines 91–98 to make this part appealing to an audience?

13 What are some of the possible snags an audience may see in Lysander's plan (lines 156–168), and in Hermia telling Helena about the plan (lines 202–221)?

5 Contexts and responses

Shakespeare took stories from various sources to turn them into plays. Sometimes he kept the setting of the original source because it provided a useful context, such as ancient Athens with its laws about death or life as a nun as punishment for disobeying a father. Sometimes, he added a setting, such as the mysterious wood in which the events take place. The supernatural world of fairies in the wood gives scope to use exotic costume, props, music and movement to create a magical world. Shakespeare's language helps to create a *context within the play* of ancient Athens by reference to characters and events the audience will recognise from classical history and stories.

14 In what ways does Shakespeare establish the play is set in ancient Athens (lines 89, 169, 171 and 173–174)?

15 How might directors of a stage version and a screen version approach the opening scene using the advantages of the technologies available to them?

16 In what ways might different people over time feel unsympathetic or a degree of understanding towards Egeus as a father disappointed by his daughter's choice of partner and angry because of her disobedience?

17 What difference would it make to the way Hermia's refusal to marry Demetrius is played if the director chose to set the play in the modern world?

6 Reflecting on the scene

18 What do you think are the themes and ideas introduced in this scene to be developed in the rest of the play?

19 How does Shakespeare present the relationship between Hermia and Helena in lines 180–223 in this scene?

20 In what ways has your response to this scene been influenced by performance on stage, on screen or in the classroom?

The Mechanicals, 2008.

This photograph was taken around line 10. Which of the men is playing Peter Quince? Give three reasons for your answer.

Paul Hunter
Bottom, 2008

The play really matters to this group of people. And hopefully that is where the comedy lies. I think the stakes have got to be very high; for them it is a huge thing to perform this play in front of the Duke. And the more serious they are about it, particularly Bottom, the more he sees himself as this really heroic actor, the bigger the gap between how he sees himself and how the world sees him is. That is where the comedy lies. They don't want to be bad. They want to be really good – it is just that they don't quite have the wherewithal to be good.

SHAKESPEARE'S WORLD

Workmen performing plays

Skilled workmen like Bottom and Quince often performed in amateur plays in medieval and Tudor England. They belonged to guilds. Each guild was an organisation of workers in just one trade, such as weavers (like Bottom) or carpenters (like Quince). Only members of the guild could follow that trade.

From the medieval period onward, the guilds of many English cities held annual religious *mystery play* cycles. These were Bible stories performed as short plays – each play acted by a different guild. These mystery plays were dying out during Queen Elizabeth's reign, and Shakespeare does make fun of his amateur actors. There were many other amateur actors in Shakespeare's time – we know of performances at universities, in country houses, and even on an English ship, the *Hector*, where a performance of *Hamlet* took place off the coast of West Africa in 1607.

ACT 1 SCENE 2

Enter Quince (the carpenter), Snug (the joiner), Bottom (the weaver), Flute (the bellows mender), Snout (the tinker), and Starveling (the tailor).

Quince	Is all our company here?
Bottom	You were best to call them generally, man by man, according to the scrip.
Quince	Here is the scroll of every man's name, which is thought fit through all Athens, to play in our interlude before the Duke and the Duchess, on his wedding day at night.
Bottom	First, good Peter Quince, say what the play treats on, then read the names of the actors, and so grow to a point.
Quince	Marry, our play is, *The most lamentable comedy, and most cruel death of Pyramus and Thisbe*.
Bottom	A very good piece of work, I assure you, and a merry. Now, good Peter Quince, call forth your actors by the scroll. Masters, spread yourselves.
Quince	Answer as I call you. Nick Bottom, the weaver.
Bottom	Ready. Name what part I am for, and proceed.
Quince	You, Nick Bottom, are set down for Pyramus.
Bottom	What is Pyramus? A lover, or a tyrant?
Quince	A lover that kills himself, most gallantly, for love.
Bottom	That will ask some tears in the true performing of it. If I do it, let the audience look to their eyes. I will move storms; I will condole in some measure. To the rest — yet my chief humour is for a tyrant. I could play Ercles rarely, or a part to tear a cat in, to make all split.

     The raging rocks
     And shivering shocks
     Shall break the locks
     Of prison gates.
     And Phibbus' car
     Shall shine from far
     And make and mar
     The foolish Fates.

    This was lofty. Now, name the rest of the players. This is Ercles' vein, a tyrant's vein. A lover is more condoling.

Quince	Francis Flute, the bellows-mender.
Flute	Here, Peter Quince.
Quince	Flute, you must take Thisbe on you.
Flute	What is Thisbe? a wandering knight?
Quince	It is the lady that Pyramus must love.

5

10

15

20

25

30

35

Notes

1 **company:** group of actors
2 **generally:** he means 'severally' – one at a time (Bottom uses many malapropisms – words used wrongly)
3 **scrip:** list
5 **interlude:** short play
6 **before:** in front of

8 **treats on:** is about
9 **grow to a point:** reach your summing-up
10 **Marry:** 'by the Virgin Mary', used at the start of a sentence for emphasis as 'well' is now
10 *lamentable:* sad
11 *Pyramus and Thisbe:* tragic lovers in a famous story
14 **spread yourselves:** spread out

20 **ask:** call for
21 **look to their eyes:** be prepared to be moved to tears
22 **condole:** show great sorrow
23 **my chief humour is for:** I'd rather play
23 **Ercles:** the Greek hero Hercules (who was not a tyrant)
24 **rarely:** amazingly well
24 **to tear a cat in:** for ranting and raging
24 **to make all split:** for going to pieces
29 **Phibbus' car:** the chariot of Phoebus Apollo, the Greek sun god
31 **mar:** ruin
32 **Fates:** three women in the myths of many cultures who controlled human life
33 **lofty:** impressive, grand
34 **vein:** way of carrying on

38 **wandering knight:** knight travelling in search of adventure

A

SHAKESPEARE'S WORLD

Boys and men playing women

There were no female actors in Shakespeare's theatre, with women only appearing on the English stage after 1660. Instead, Shakespeare's company, and all their rivals, used boy actors to play most female roles, whilst some male actors specialised in playing older women.

The boys were apprentices, learning their trade from the adult company members. Their female roles could be demanding, with many lines to learn, and long speeches to deliver. Their characters were often involved in the most dramatic scenes in the play. When they got too old to play the women's roles, they usually became male actors in the company.

Theatregoers at the time saw this as normal. Eyewitness accounts of Shakespeare's company performing simply describe the woman characters as female, without mentioning that they were played by boys and men.

Moments during the discussion of the play. *A* and *B* 2012; *C* 2008.

Which lines below were being said as each photograph was taken?
Give reasons for your answer.

1 'Ah, Pyramus, my lover dear'

2 'or your French-crown-colour beard'

3 'Nay, faith, let not me play a woman'.

Peter Bray, Russell Layton, Paul Hunter

B

C

Flute	Nay, faith, let not me play a woman. I have a beard coming.

40

Quince	That's all one. You shall play it in a mask, and you may speak as small as you will.

42 **That's all one:** it doesn't matter
42 **you may:** you need to
43 **as small as you will:** as high-pitched as you can
44 **An:** if

Bottom	An I may hide my face, let me play Thisbe too. I'll speak in a monstrous little voice. "Thisne, Thisne! " — "Ah, Pyramus, my lover dear, thy Thisbe dear, and lady dear."

45

Quince	No, no, you must play Pyramus — and Flute, you Thisbe.
Bottom	Well, proceed.
Quince	Robin Starveling, the tailor.

50

Starveling	Here, Peter Quince.
Quince	Robin Starveling, you must play Thisbe's mother. — Tom Snout, the tinker.
Snout	Here, Peter Quince.
Quince	You, Pyramus' father; myself, Thisbe's father. Snug, the joiner, you, the lion's part. And I hope here is a play fitted.

55

57 **fitted:** well-cast

Snug	Have you the lion's part written? Pray you, if it be, give it me, for I am slow of study.

59 **of study:** to learn things

Quince	You may do it extempore, for it is nothing but roaring.

60

60 **extempore:** without a script

Bottom	Let me play the lion too. I will roar, that I will do any man's heart good to hear me. I will roar, that I will make the Duke say, "Let him roar again, let him roar again."

Quince	If you should do it too terribly, you would fright the Duchess and the ladies, that they would shriek, and that were enough to hang us all.

65

All	That would hang us, every mother's son.

Bottom	I grant you, friends, if you should fright the ladies out of their wits, they would have no more discretion but to hang us. But I will aggravate my voice so, that I will roar you as gently as any sucking dove; I will roar you an 'twere any nightingale.

70

70 **no more discretion:** he means 'no choice', but he's saying 'no judgement'
71 **aggravate:** he means 'moderate'
72 **sucking dove:** he confuses two phrases for gentleness: 'sitting dove' and 'sucking lamb'
73 **an 'twere:** as if it was

Quince	You can play no part but Pyramus, for Pyramus is a sweet-faced man, a proper man, as one shall see in a summer's day, a most lovely gentleman-like man. Therefore you must needs play Pyramus.

75

Bottom	Well, I will undertake it. What beard were I best to play it in?

Quince	Why, what you will.

80

80 **what you will:** it's up to you
81 **discharge:** play
82 **purple-in-grain:** deep red
83 **French-crown-colour:** deep red

Bottom	I will discharge it in either your straw-colour beard, your orange-tawny beard, your purple-in-grain beard, or your French-crown-colour beard, your perfect yellow.

23

A

B

Director's Note, 1.2

✔ A group of workmen from Athens meet to plan the play they want to perform to celebrate the Duke's marriage.

✔ Peter Quince gives each actor his part, and they plan to meet in the woods the next night to rehearse.

A Flute, Bottom, Quince, Starveling, Snout, Snug (partly hidden), 2008.

l–r Peter Bankolé, Paul Hunter, Michael Matus, Sam Parks, Jonathan Bond, Robert Goodale

B Starveling, Bottom, Flute, Quince, Snout, Snug, 2002.

l–r Ryan Early, John Ramm, Aled Pugh, Paul Trussell, Patrick Lennox, Jem Wall

These photographs both show moments during Quince's speech on the opposite page. Which photograph shows the earlier part of the action during the speech? Give reasons for your answer.

SHAKESPEARE'S WORLD

Cue scripts

Actors in Shakespeare's time did not have a complete copy of the play. Each got his own part, handwritten, with just his lines, and his *cue* – the very end of the last line before each of his speeches. Actors relied on these cues of one to three words to know when it was their turn to speak. This meant that each actor knew little about what other characters were saying or doing until they rehearsed, and they had to listen to the other actors very closely. These scripts are the *parts* Quince hands out, normally written on long strips of paper.

SHAKESPEARE'S WORLD

Fairies

In Shakespeare's day, it was common to believe in fairies or spirits. These creatures were magical beings that had no souls but could interact with humans. Fairies were considered ugly like goblins or elves. Elizabethans thought that fairies could change shape and size at any time. Usually, they would be the size of small children. At times, they could even be as small as ants. The fairies in the play are small enough to crawl around in acorn cups. They are named after items that are small, like cobwebs and mustard seeds. Titania's Fairies were probably originally played by small boy actors. People believed they could also fly, become invisible, and enjoyed riding, hunting and dancing. They also liked eating great feasts and sometimes even stole food. Fairies ate beef and bread, but they loved milk and cream. People thought that fairies punished men and women for behaving badly. If a house was messy, fairies would play tricks on the housewife. They hated dirt and disorder. Fairies also cursed livestock and caused disease. Sometimes they would pinch people or steal their children.

Quince	Some of your French crowns have no hair at all, and then you will play bare-faced. But masters, here are your parts. *[Handing out scripts.]* And I am to entreat you, request you, and desire you, to con them by tomorrow night, and meet me in the palace wood, a mile without the town, by moonlight. There will we rehearse, for if we meet in the city we shall be dogged with company, and our devices known. In the meantime I will draw a bill of properties, such as our play wants. I pray you, fail me not.
Bottom	We will meet, and there we may rehearse most obscenely and courageously. Take pains. Be perfect. Adieu.
Quince	At the Duke's Oak we meet.
Bottom	Enough. Hold or cut bow-strings.

They exit.

ACT 2 SCENE 1

Enter a Fairy at one door and Puck at another.

Puck	How now spirit, whither wander you?
Fairy	Over hill, over dale,
	Thorough bush, thorough brier,
	Over park, over pale,
	Thorough flood, thorough fire,
	I do wander everywhere,
	Swifter than the moon's sphere;
	And I serve the Fairy Queen,
	To dew her orbs upon the green.
	The cowslips tall, her pensioners be,
	In their gold coats, spots you see,
	Those be rubies, fairy favours,
	In those freckles live their savours.
	I must go seek some dewdrops here
	And hang a pearl in every cowslip's ear.
	Farewell thou lob of spirits, I'll be gone,
	Our Queen and all her elves come here anon.
Puck	The king doth keep his revels here tonight.
	Take heed the Queen come not within his sight,
	For Oberon is passing fell and wrath,
	Because that she, as her attendant, hath
	A lovely boy stolen from an Indian king.
	She never had so sweet a changeling
	And jealous Oberon would have the child
	Knight of his train, to trace the forests wild.
	But she, perforce, withholds the lovèd boy,
	Crowns him with flowers, and makes him all her joy.
	And now they never meet in grove or green,
	By fountain clear, or spangled starlight sheen,
	But they do square, that all their elves for fear
	Creep into acorn-cups and hide them there.

Line numbers: 85, 90, 95 (left column); 5, 10, 15, 20, 25, 30 (Act 2 Scene 1).

84 Some of your ... no hair at all: Some Frenchmen are bald (a reference to syphilis, which was called 'the French disease' and caused baldness)

87 con: learn

89 without: outside

90–1 we shall be dogged with company: all sorts of people will follow us to watch

91 devices: plans

92–3 draw a bill of properties ... play wants: make a list of the props we need

95 obscenely: he means 'obscurely' – secretly

95 Take pains: make an effort

95 Be perfect: learn your parts thoroughly

98 Hold or cut bow-strings: keep your word or be disgraced (an archer's saying, stand and fight or give up)

3 Thorough: through

4 park: enclosed hunting grounds

4 pale: fence

7 sphere: orbit

9 orbs upon the green: fairy rings (dark circles) in the grass

10 her pensioners be: are her bodyguards

12 favours: gifts

13 savours: scent

16 thou lob of spirits: you loutish spirit

17 anon: any minute now

18 doth keep his revels: is bringing his court

19 Take heed: make sure

20 passing fell: very bitter

20 wrath: angry

23 changeling: a human child swapped at birth by fairies

25 Knight of his train: one of his followers

25 trace: wander through

26 perforce: forcibly

29 fountain: spring where a river or stream begins

29 spangled starlight sheen: in the bright, glittering starlight

30 square: quarrel

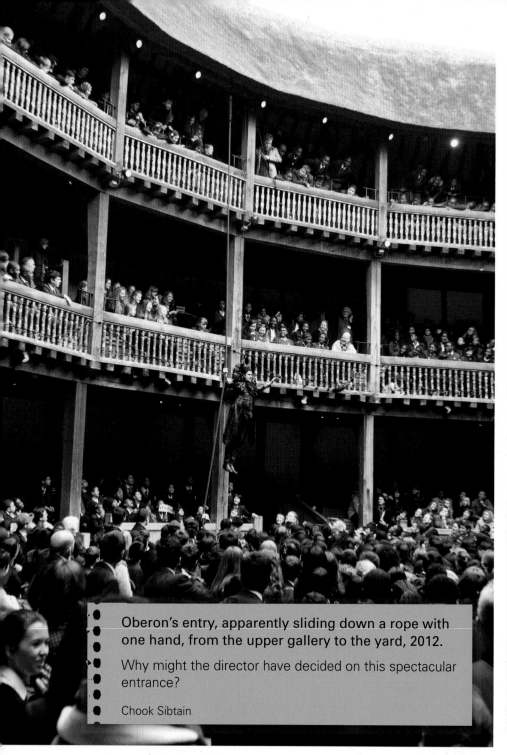

Oberon's entry, apparently sliding down a rope with one hand, from the upper gallery to the yard, 2012.

Why might the director have decided on this spectacular entrance?

Chook Sibtain

Robin Goodfellow/Puck

In this scene, we meet Puck, one of the higher-ranking Fairies to serve Oberon. Puck, or Robin Goodfellow, was part of England's fairy mythology. Shakespeare's first audiences would recognise his name. There were many ballads or songs written about him. He was a fairy, but not the tiny, winged kind that we often imagine.

He was mischievous. In the stories, he was a *shape-changer*. He could turn himself into something else – things like a stool, a hare, a ghost, or different people. He used this skill to play tricks on people, like the stories about housewives and maidservants he mentions here. But he was also sometimes frightening. People associated him with demons and other scary creatures. He would steal children and make loved ones disappear. One sixteenth-century writer, who tried hard to convince people that witchcraft and fairies were old wives' tales, mentions Robin Goodfellow and says that 'our mothers' maids have so terrified us with an ugly devil who has horns on his head'. So stories about Puck might have been made up to keep children well-behaved. Shakespeare links his Puck to this tradition, but he also makes him unique. His Puck is mischievous and naughty, but we like him. He seems almost human, even though he mocks the Athenians for being foolish mortals.

Actor's view

Siobhan Redmond
Titania, 2008

The relationship between Titania and Oberon is much nastier. They definitely fancy each other, but I think their relationship is always going to be fraught. In this play, it is a happy ending for them, but you know that the next day there will be something else. Normally when you see this play the Indian boy is referred to, but he isn't seen much. But my Indian boy is going to be with me quite a lot of the time, until Titania falls in love with Bottom. I've not seen that done before, and it will be fun to see what the audience makes of seeing the poor child being shut out of the bower.

Actor's view

Chook Sibtain
Oberon, 2012

She gives a lot of attention to the Indian boy. Oberon makes reference to her devoting her time and energy to the boy and making him the object of all her desires, and I think there's a great deal of jealousy there. Oberon is very petulant and spoilt in many ways. She denies him the boy, so he has to have him. Not to use in any practical way but to parade – Oberon says he would make him 'the knight of all his train', just to show off to all the rest of the fairy kingdom that he's the man. It's a bit of a red herring really, the Indian boy, because by the end it doesn't matter anyway. It could be anything.

Fairy	Either I mistake your shape and making quite,
	Or else you are that shrewd and knavish sprite
	Called Robin Goodfellow. Are not you he
	That frights the maidens of the villag'ry 35
	Skim milk, and sometimes labour in the quern
	And bootless make the breathless housewife churn,
	And sometime make the drink to bear no barm,
	Mislead night-wand'rers, laughing at their harm?
	Those that "Hobgoblin" call you, and "sweet Puck", 40
	You do their work, and they shall have good luck.
	Are not you he?
Puck	Thou speak'st aright,
	I am that merry wand'rer of the night.
	I jest to Oberon and make him smile
	When I a fat and bean-fed horse beguile, 45
	Neighing in likeness of a filly foal.
	And sometime lurk I in a gossip's bowl,
	In very likeness of a roasted crab,
	And when she drinks, against her lips I bob,
	And on her withered dewlap pour the ale. 50
	The wisest aunt telling the saddest tale,
	Sometime for three-foot stool mistaketh me,
	Then slip I from her bum, down topples she,
	And "tailor" cries, and falls into a cough.
	And then the whole choir hold their hips and laugh, 55
	And waxen in their mirth, and sneeze, and swear
	A merrier hour was never wasted there.
	But room, Fairy! Here comes Oberon.
Fairy	And here my mistress. Would that he were gone!

*Enter Oberon with his attendants at one door, and Titania
with her attendants at another.*

Oberon	Ill met by moonlight, proud Titania. 60
Titania	What, jealous Oberon? Fairies skip hence:
	I have forsworn his bed and company.
Oberon	Tarry, rash wanton. Am not I thy lord?
Titania	Then I must be thy lady. But I know
	When thou hast stol'n away from Fairy Land, 65
	And in the shape of Corin sat all day,
	Playing on pipes of corn and versing love
	To amorous Phillida. Why art thou here,
	Come from the farthest step of India?
	But that, forsooth, the bouncing Amazon, 70
	Your buskined mistress and your warrior love,
	To Theseus must be wedded; and you come
	To give their bed joy and prosperity?
Oberon	How canst thou thus, for shame Titania,
	Glance at my credit with Hippolyta, 75
	Knowing I know thy love to Theseus?
	Didst not thou lead him through the glimmering night
	From Perigenia, whom he ravishèd?

32 **making:** physical appearance
32 **quite:** entirely
33 **shrewd:** malicious, spiteful
33 **knavish:** deceitful
35 **villag'ry:** villagers
36 **Skim milk:** takes the cream from the top of the milk
36 **quern:** normally used to grind corn, but here it means a butter churn
37 **bootless:** unrewarded
37 **churn:** work the butter-making churn
38 **the drink:** beer
38 **barm:** frothy head
39 **Mislead night-wand'rers:** lead those travelling at night astray
41 **their work:** but you do jobs for them
44 **jest to:** tell jokes to
45 **beguile:** trick
46 **in likeness of a filly foal:** just like a young female horse
47 **gossip:** nosy old woman
48 **crab:** crab apple
50 **withered dewlap:** loose, wrinkled skin at the neck
51 **aunt:** old woman
54 **"tailor":** 'bum' ('tail' was another word for 'bum')
55 **the whole choir:** all her friends
56 **waxen in their mirth:** laugh harder
58 **room:** out of the way

62 **forsworn:** sworn to avoid
63 **Tarry:** wait
63 **rash wanton:** headstrong, unfaithful woman
63 **thy lord:** your husband
64 **thy lady:** your wife
66 **Corin:** a handsome shepherd in stories
67 **pipes of corn:** musical instruments made from hollow corn stalks
68 **Phillida:** courted by Corin (note line 66)
70 **the bouncing Amazon:** Hippolyta
71 **buskined:** wearing buskins – a kind of boot
75 **Glance at my credit with:** make accusations to me about

GLOBAL WARMING

In her speech (lines 81–117) Titania talks about the effects of her quarrel with Oberon on the world in which they live.

- In groups, suggest six words that describe late spring/early summer and collect those into a list.

- Now read Titania's speech and make a list of all the words which describe how the natural world is suffering from unusual events.

- Take it turns to read the words out and use your voice to explore different ways of saying them. What is the best way of saying them?

1 Fold a sheet of paper in half and put the titles 'Before the Quarrel' in one half and 'During the Quarrel' in the other. Using the two lists you have made, quickly draw a picture of the different scenes and add the words around and in your drawings.

2 As a group, devise the headline and the opening paragraph of a front page story on the unusual weather and farming conditions.

SHAKESPEARE'S WORLD
◇◇◇◇◇◇◇◇◇◇◇◇

A changeling

A changeling is a child who has been swapped for another child. Elizabethans believed that fairies might take a pretty baby and leave behind an ugly one. This was one way of punishing humans for bad behaviour. In the play, Titania's changeling boy has been taken from India. Oberon claims the boy was a prince and was stolen by the Fairies. Titania says that his mother died in childbirth.

SHAKESPEARE'S WORLD
◇◇◇◇◇◇◇◇◇◇◇◇

Weather lore

The superstitious members of Shakespeare's audience believed the weather reflected what would happen in their lives. Obviously, the right weather was important for growing food. The Elizabethans knew that bad weather could mean bad harvest and starvation. Some took this much further. For example, believing thunder on Monday meant a woman would die, while thunder on Thursday promised lots of sheep. Some people believed that this happened because of magic people or creatures. Titania's lines reflect these superstitions. She says to Oberon that the terrible weather has happened because they have been fighting.

Titania, the Indian boy, and the Fairies, 2008.

Compare this photo with the one on page 12 (both 2008 production). Describe how the look has changed from Athens to the Fairies in the wood and the effect it might have on the audience.

And make him with fair Aegles break his faith,
With Ariadne and Antiope? 80

Titania
These are the forgeries of jealousy.
And never, since the middle summer's spring
Met we on hill, in dale, forest, or mead,
By pavèd fountain, or by rushy brook,
Or in the beachèd margent of the sea, 85
To dance our ringlets to the whistling wind,
But with thy brawls thou hast disturbed our sport.
Therefore the winds, piping to us in vain,
As in revenge, have sucked up from the sea
Contagious fogs, which falling in the land, 90
Hath every petty river made so proud
That they have overborne their continents.
The ox hath therefore stretched his yoke in vain,
The ploughman lost his sweat, and the green corn
Hath rotted ere his youth attained a beard. 95
The fold stands empty in the drownèd field,
And crows are fatted with the murrion flock,
The Nine Men's Morris is filled up with mud,
And the quaint mazes in the wanton green,
For lack of tread are undistinguishable. 100
The human mortals want their winter cheer,
No night is now with hymn or carol blest.
Therefore the moon (the governess of floods)
Pale in her anger, washes all the air,
That rheumatic diseases do abound. 105
And thorough this distemperature we see
The seasons alter, hoary-headed frosts
Fall in the fresh lap of the crimson rose,
And on old Hiems' thin and icy crown
An odorous chaplet of sweet summer buds 110
Is, as in mockery, set. The spring, the summer,
The childing autumn, angry winter, change
Their wonted liveries, and the mazèd world
By their increase, now knows not which is which.
And this same progeny of evils comes 115
From our debate, from our dissension.
We are their parents and original.

Oberon
Do you amend it then, it lies in you.
Why should Titania cross her Oberon?
I do but beg a little changeling boy, 120
To be my henchman.

Titania
                    Set your heart at rest,
The Fairy Land buys not the child of me.
His mother was a votress of my order,
And, in the spicèd Indian air, by night
Full often hath she gossiped by my side, 125
And sat with me on Neptune's yellow sands,
Marking th' embarkèd traders on the flood,
When we have laughed to see the sails conceive
And grow big-bellied with the wanton wind.

78–80 Perigenia … Aegles … Ariadne … Antiope: all women Theseus made love to, then abandoned
81 the forgeries of jealousy: jealous imaginings
82 spring: beginning
83 mead: grassy field
84 pavèd fountain: pebble-bottomed spring
84 rushy brook: stream lined with rushes
85 margent: edge
86 dance our ringlets: dance in a circle
87 brawls: quarrelling
90 Contagious: disease-spreading
91 petty: small
92 overborne their continents: overflowed
93 stretched his yoke: pulled the plough
94 green: unripe
95 his youth attained a beard: it ripened
96 fold: sheep enclosure
97 are fatted with: eat
97 murrion flock: diseased sheep
99 quaint mazes: complicated paths
99 wanton green: lush grass
101 want: have to do without
103 Therefore: because of our dispute
103 governess of floods: ruler of the tides
106 distemperature: disordered weather
107 hoary-headed: white-haired
109 Hiems: the personification of winter
110 odorous: scented
110 chaplet: crown of flowers
112 childing: fertile
113 wonted liveries: usual uniform
113 mazèd: confused
114 their increase: what they produce
115 this same progeny of evils: all these bad consequences
116 dissension: disagreement
117 original: where they come from
118 Do you amend it: you put it right
123 a votress of my order: one of my female followers
125 Full often: many times
126 Neptune: Roman god of the sea
127 Marking: watching
127 th' embarkèd traders: the loaded trading ships
127 the flood: the sea
128 conceive: fill out, as if pregnant
129 wanton: lustful

Puck and Oberon, 2008.

Do you think this photo was taken before or after Titania's exit? Quote from the text to support your answer.

Michael Jibson, Tom Mannion

FROM THE REHEARSAL ROOM...

THE CLASH

- In pairs, cast yourselves as Titania and Oberon and read through the *Working Cut*.
- Read it again but, this time, listen very carefully and repeat the most important word or phrase the character before has said, then speak your own lines.
- Note the words or phrases you picked out.
- Read the scene again, only this time when you repeat the word or phrase think how it might affect your character.

1 What does Oberon want from Titania?

2 Why will she not give him what he wants?

3 Is there more than one reason for their argument? If so, list the reasons in order of importance.

4 List three characteristics that you think Oberon and Titania display in this argument. Quote from the text to support your answer.

Working Cut – text for experiment

Ob   Ill met by moonlight, proud Titania.

Tita   What, jealous Oberon? Fairies skip hence:
I have forsworn his bed and company.

Ob   Tarry, rash wanton. Am not I thy lord?

Tita   Then I must be thy lady. But I know
When thou hast stol'n away from Fairy Land,
And in the shape of Corin sat all day,
Playing on pipes of corn and versing love
To amorous Phillida. Why art thou here,
Come from the farthest step of India?
But that, forsooth, the bouncing Amazon,
Your buskined mistress and your warrior love,
To Theseus must be wedded; and you come
To give their bed joy and prosperity?

Ob   How canst thou thus, for shame Titania,
Glance at my credit with Hippolyta,
Knowing I know thy love to Theseus?

Tita   These are the forgeries of jealousy.
And never, since the middle summer's spring
Met we on hill, in dale, forest, or mead,
By pavèd fountain, or by rushy brook,
Or in the beachèd margent of the sea,
To dance our ringlets to the whistling wind,
But with thy brawls thou hast disturbed our sport.

Ob   Do you amend it then, it lies in you.
Why should Titania cross her Oberon?
I do but beg a little changeling boy,
To be my henchman.

Tita   Set your heart at rest,
The Fairy Land buys not the child of me.
His mother was a votress of my order,
And, in the spicèd Indian air, by night
Full often hath she gossiped by my side,
But she, being mortal, of that boy did die,
And for her sake do I rear up her boy,
And for her sake I will not part with him.

Ob   How long within this wood intend you stay?

Tita   Perchance till after Theseus' wedding day.
If you will patiently dance in our round
And see our moonlight revels, go with us.
If not, shun me and I will spare your haunts.

Ob   Give me that boy, and I will go with thee.

Tita   Not for thy Fairy Kingdom. Fairies, away!
We shall chide downright if I longer stay.
Exit Titania and her attendants.

Ob   Well, go thy way. Thou shalt not from this grove
Till I torment thee for this injury.

	Which she, with pretty and with swimming gait,	130
	Following (her womb then rich with my young squire)	
	Would imitate, and sail upon the land	
	To fetch me trifles, and return again,	
	As from a voyage, rich with merchandise.	
	But she, being mortal, of that boy did die,	135
	And for her sake do I rear up her boy,	
	And for her sake I will not part with him.	

Oberon   How long within this wood intend you stay?

Titania   Perchance till after Theseus' wedding day.
If you will patiently dance in our round   140
And see our moonlight revels, go with us.
If not, shun me and I will spare your haunts.

Oberon   Give me that boy, and I will go with thee.

Titania   Not for thy Fairy Kingdom. Fairies, away!
We shall chide downright if I longer stay.   145

Exit Titania and her attendants.

Oberon   Well, go thy way. Thou shalt not from this grove
Till I torment thee for this injury.
My gentle Puck come hither. Thou rememb'rest
Since once I sat upon a promontory
And heard a mermaid, on a dolphin's back,   150
Uttering such dulcet and harmonious breath
That the rude sea grew civil at her song,
And certain stars shot madly from their spheres
To hear the sea-maid's music?

Puck   I remember.

Oberon   That very time I saw (but thou couldst not)   155
Flying between the cold moon and the earth,
Cupid all armed. A certain aim he took
At a fair vestal, thronèd by the west,
And loosed his love-shaft smartly from his bow
As it should pierce a hundred thousand hearts.   160
But I might see young Cupid's fiery shaft
Quenched in the chaste beams of the wat'ry moon,
And the imperial votress passèd on,
In maiden meditation, fancy-free.
Yet marked I where the bolt of Cupid fell.   165
It fell upon a little western flower,
Before, milk-white, now purple with love's wound,
And maidens call it love-in-idleness.
Fetch me that flower, the herb I showed thee once.
The juice of it on sleeping eye-lids laid   170
Will make or man or woman madly dote
Upon the next live creature that it sees.
Fetch me this herb, and be thou here again
Ere the leviathan can swim a league.

Puck   I'll put a girdle round about the earth   175
In forty minutes.   *[Exit Puck.]*

---

130 **swimming gait:** graceful movements

133 **trifles:** small presents

135 **of that boy did die:** died giving birth to the boy

139 **Perchance:** probably
140 **patiently:** calmly

142 **shun:** avoid
142 **spare your haunts:** keep out of your way

145 **chide downright:** fall out completely
146 **go thy way:** do as you please
146 **from:** leave

149 **Since:** when
149 **promontory:** headland
151 **Uttering such dulcet and harmonious breath:** singing so beautifully
152 **rude:** rough
152 **civil:** gentle
153 **spheres:** orbits

157 **all:** fully
157 **certain:** sure
158 **vestal:** virgin
158 **thronèd by:** ruling in
159 **love-shaft:** arrow
160 **As:** as if
161 **I might see:** I could see
162 **Quenched:** I put out
163 **imperial votress:** ruler dedicated to chastity
164 **fancy-free:** without falling in love
165 **marked I:** I noticed
165 **the bolt:** the arrow
168 **love-in-idleness:** a flower, pansy, also called 'heartsease'
171 **or ... or:** either ... or
171-2 **dote Upon:** fall madly in love with

174 **leviathan:** huge sea monster
175 **girdle:** belt
175 **round about:** around

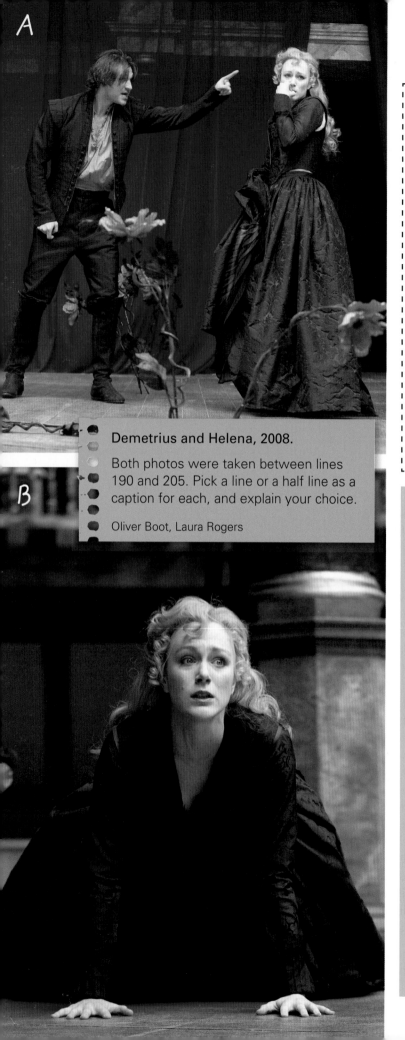

A

B

Demetrius and Helena, 2008.

Both photos were taken between lines 190 and 205. Pick a line or a half line as a caption for each, and explain your choice.

Oliver Boot, Laura Rogers

Working Cut – text for experiment

Dem	I love thee not, therefore pursue me not.
Hel	You draw me, you hard-hearted adamant,
Dem	Do I entice you? Do I speak you fair?
	Or, rather, do I not in plainest truth
	Tell you, I do not, nor I cannot love you?
Hel	And even for that do I love thee the more.
	I am your spaniel, and, Demetrius,
	The more you beat me, I will fawn on you.
Dem	Tempt not too much the hatred of my spirit,
	For I am sick when I do look on thee.
Hel	And I am sick when I look not on you.
Dem	You do impeach your modesty too much,
	To leave the city and commit yourself
	Into the hands of one that loves you not,
	To trust the opportunity of night,
	And the ill counsel of a desert place,
	With the rich worth of your virginity.
Hel	Your virtue is my privilege. For that
	It is not night when I do see your face
Dem	I'll run from thee and hide me in the brakes,
	And leave thee to the mercy of wild beasts.
Hel	The wildest hath not such a heart as you.
Dem	I will not stay thy questions. Let me go!
	Or if thou follow me, do not believe
	But I shall do thee mischief in the wood.
Hel	Ay, in the temple, in the town, the field,
	You do me mischief.

Oberon	Having once this juice, I'll watch Titania when she is asleep, And drop the liquor of it in her eyes. The next thing then she waking looks upon, (Be it on lion, bear, or wolf, or bull, On meddling monkey, or on busy ape) She shall pursue it with the soul of love. And ere I take this charm from off her sight, (As I can take it with another herb) I'll make her render up her page to me. — But who comes here? I am invisible, And I will overhear their conference.

180

182 **pursue it with the soul of love:** fall madly in love with it
183 **ere:** before

185 **render up:** give

187 **conference:** conversation

Enter Demetrius, then Helena following him.

Demetrius	I love thee not, therefore pursue me not. Where is Lysander and fair Hermia? The one I'll stay, the other stayeth me. Thou told'st me they were stol'n unto this wood, And here am I, and wood within this wood Because I cannot meet my Hermia. Hence, get thee gone, and follow me no more.
Helena	You draw me, you hard-hearted adamant, But yet you draw not iron, for my heart Is true as steel. Leave you your power to draw, And I shall have no power to follow you.
Demetrius	Do I entice you? Do I speak you fair? Or, rather, do I not in plainest truth Tell you, I do not, nor I cannot love you?
Helena	And even for that do I love thee the more. I am your spaniel, and, Demetrius, The more you beat me, I will fawn on you. Use me but as your spaniel, spurn me, strike me, Neglect me, lose me; only give me leave (Unworthy as I am) to follow you. What worser place can I beg in your love, (And yet a place of high respect with me) Than to be used as you use your dog?
Demetrius	Tempt not too much the hatred of my spirit, For I am sick when I do look on thee.
Helena	And I am sick when I look not on you.
Demetrius	You do impeach your modesty too much, To leave the city and commit yourself Into the hands of one that loves you not, To trust the opportunity of night, And the ill counsel of a desert place, With the rich worth of your virginity.
Helena	Your virtue is my privilege. For that It is not night when I do see your face, Therefore I think I am not in the night. Nor doth this wood lack worlds of company,

190
190 **The one I'll stay:** I'll stop one
190 **the other stayeth me:** the other is what keeps me here
192 **wood:** driven to fury

194 **Hence:** leave here
195 **draw me:** pull me to you
195 195 **adamant:** both a magnet and a very hard metal
197 **Leave you:** give up

199 **speak you fair:** talk to you kindly
200

203 **spaniel:** a breed of dog famous for being faithful even if ill-treated
204 **fawn on:** lavish love on
205 **Use me but as:** treat me just like
205 205 **spurn me:** push me away
206 **leave:** permission

210

211 **Tempt not ... of my spirit:** don't push your luck

214 **You do impeach ... too much:** you're putting your reputation to too great a test
215

218 **the ill counsel of a desert place:** in a desolate place where you can't call for help

220 220 **Your virtue is my privilege:** I'm safe with you, you are a good man
220 **For that:** because

33

Puck and Oberon, 2012.

In this production Puck did not give Oberon the flower straight away, but kept turning away from him. He even got out a water pistol to water it. What is there in the text which encouraged this interpretation? Quote from the text to support your answer.

Fergal McElherron, Chook Sibtain

FROM THE REHEARSAL ROOM...

DRUGWATCH

A *Midsummer Night's Dream* is a comedy, so we laugh at the confusion caused by the use of the flower. If it was a different sort of play, we might think of the use of drugs to change people's beliefs and behaviour as rather sinister. This is a series of activities that run throughout the play. The instructions in blue are used every time you do *Drugwatch*.

- This is a role-play. Cast the Investigator, Puck, Oberon, and one or more Observers.

- Puck and Oberon (the Witnesses) should study from line 246 to the end of the scene carefully.

- The Investigator interrogates the witnesses, to find the answers to the numbered questions below (and evidence to support the answers), but cannot use these actual words. While the Witnesses study their text the Investigator and Observers should work out the best questions.

- The Witnesses must answer truthfully.

- The observers can challenge any answer they think is wrong.

- After your role-play, write up the Investigator's Report (answer the questions).

1 Who is the mastermind and what is the plan?

2 What are Oberon's motives?

3 What are Puck's motives?

	For you, in my respect, are all the world.
	Then how can it be said I am alone,
	When all the world is here to look on me?
Demetrius	I'll run from thee and hide me in the brakes,
	And leave thee to the mercy of wild beasts.
Helena	The wildest hath not such a heart as you.
	Run when you will, the story shall be changed:
	Apollo flies, and Daphne holds the chase;
	The dove pursues the griffin; the mild hind
	Makes speed to catch the tiger. Bootless speed,
	When cowardice pursues and valour flies.
Demetrius	I will not stay thy questions. Let me go!
	Or if thou follow me, do not believe
	But I shall do thee mischief in the wood.
Helena	Ay, in the temple, in the town, the field,
	You do me mischief. Fie, Demetrius,
	Your wrongs do set a scandal on my sex.
	We cannot fight for love, as men may do,
	We should be wooed and were not made to woo.

[Exit Demetrius.]

| | I'll follow thee, and make a heaven of hell, |
| | To die upon the hand I love so well. |

Exit Helena.

| Oberon | Fare thee well nymph. Ere he do leave this grove, |
| | Thou shalt fly him, and he shall seek thy love. |

Enter Puck.

	Hast thou the flower there? Welcome, wanderer.
Puck	Ay, there it is.
Oberon	I pray thee give it me.
	I know a bank where the wild thyme blows,
	Where oxlips and the nodding violet grows,
	Quite over-canopied with luscious woodbine,
	With sweet musk-roses and with eglantine.
	There sleeps Titania, sometime of the night,
	Lulled in these flowers with dances and delight.
	And there the snake throws her enamelled skin,
	Weed wide enough to wrap a fairy in.
	And with the juice of this I'll streak her eyes,
	And make her full of hateful fantasies.

[Gives him some of the flower.]

	Take thou some of it, and seek through this grove;
	A sweet Athenian lady is in love
	With a disdainful youth. Anoint his eyes,
	But do it when the next thing he espies
	May be the lady. Thou shalt know the man
	By the Athenian garments he hath on.
	Effect it with some care, that he may prove
	More fond on her than she upon her love.
	And look thou meet me ere the first cock crow.
Puck	Fear not my lord, your servant shall do so.

They exit.

Glossary

224 **in my respect:** to me
227 **brakes:** bushes
231 **Apollo flies:** in Greek myths, the god Apollo chased Daphne
232 **griffin:** fierce mythical animal: part lion, part eagle
232 **hind:** female deer
233 **Bootless:** pointless
234 **valour:** bravery
235 **stay:** wait for
236-7 **do not believe But:** you had better believe
237 **do thee mischief:** harm you
239 **Fie:** shame on you!
240 **Your wrongs do set ... on my sex:** the way you treat me makes me behave in a way that disgraces women
244 **To die upon:** to be killed by
245 **nymph:** lovely girl (nymphs were beautiful spirits in Greek myths)
249 **a bank:** a sheltered, sloping, piece of land
249 **blows:** blooms
251 **Quite over-canopied with:** with a thick roof of
251 **woodbine:** honeysuckle
252 **eglantine:** a wild rose
253 **sometime of:** for part of
254 **Lulled:** sent to sleep in
254 **with:** by
255 **throws:** sheds
256 **Weed:** cloth
257 **streak:** smear
258 **hateful fantasies:** unpleasant imaginings
259 **grove:** wood
261 **disdainful:** scornful
262 **espies:** sees
265 **Effect:** do
265 **that:** so that
266 **fond on:** infatuated with

Director's Note, 2.1

✔ Oberon and Titania meet in the woods and quarrel over the Indian boy. Titania refuses to give him to Oberon.

✔ Oberon plans revenge on Titania and sends Puck to find a flower that has the power to make people fall madly in love.

✔ Oberon sees Demetrius reject Helena and feels sorry for her.

✔ Puck returns with the flower. Oberon takes some of it to drug Titania, and sends Puck to find an Athenian man and woman, to drug the man.

✔ Are Oberon's orders clear?

EXAMINER'S NOTES, 2.1

These questions help you to explore many aspects of *A Midsummer Night's Dream.* Support each answer by reference to the text. At GCSE, your teacher will tell you which aspects are relevant to how your Shakespeare response will be assessed.

EXAMINER'S TIP

A good response

A good response may include more than one way of interpreting a scene. The key word is 'or'. For example, in this scene, you may think that Oberon is right to be jealous because Titania seems fonder of the Indian boy than she is of him, or you may think he is annoyed because he thinks she should obey him as her master.

USING THE VIDEO

Exploring interpretation and performance

If you have looked at the video extracts in Dynamic Learning try these questions.

'I love thee not…' (line 188).

The Globe production makes much of the comic possibilities of this scene, with Demetrius trying to escape from Helena, and she, doing spaniel impressions and pinning him down, the dominant one.

- Which character gets your sympathy in the scene?
- How does Helena's line about wooing (line 242) create ironic humour to add to the visual humour?

❶ Character and plot development

Act 1 Scene 1 established the main romantic plot of the play, the complications between the lovers Hermia, Lysander, Helena and Demetrius. Act 1 Scene 2 established the second, comic, plot of the amateur dramatics of the Athens Mechanicals. Act 2 Scene 1 establishes the third plot, the relationship between the King and Queen of the Fairies, Oberon and Titania. The scene combines the romantic and comic aspects of the other plots, and introduces the supernatural.

1 What links can you see between the two supernatural characters, Oberon and Titania, and the human characters in the play, in lines 60–81?
2 How does Shakespeare present Titania as a character in lines 121–145?
3 How does Shakespeare present Oberon as a character in lines 146–174?
4 How does Shakespeare develop Oberon's character in lines 186–187, 245–247 and 259–267?

❷ Characterisation and voice: dramatic language

Shakespeare's imagery conveys ideas, feelings and attitudes by reference to things that the audience is familiar with. It draws on knowledge of plants to create a realistic setting, on knowledge of classical mythology and on knowledge of agriculture. His audience would be familiar with most of this, so his imagery draws on common experience.

5 Titania accuses Oberon of being jealous but shows signs of jealousy herself. How is their jealousy shown as affecting the world of nature in lines 81–117?
6 How is Oberon's speech in lines 148–154 used to create a contrast with the destructive effects described by Titania?

❸ Themes and ideas

Shakespeare presents love as a powerful force that does not always 'run smooth', and not only with the mortal characters. He also makes humans seem influenced by other forces that affect how 'smooth' life runs, such as the supernatural. He introduces dreams and sleep as aspects where the supernatural can intervene and transform, with Oberon's plan for the 'love potion'.

7 How does Shakespeare use Puck to create similarities between the emotions of characters from the supernatural world and the world of human beings in lines 18–31?
8 How does Shakespeare present the power of supernatural beings to influence the human world in lines 32–57?
9 What aspects of love does Shakespeare present in this scene in lines 188–244?
10 Do you think Shakespeare shows Helena's love for Demetrius as a strength or a weakness in lines 188–244?
11 In what ways does Shakespeare use dreams and sleep as aspects where the supernatural can intervene and transform in lines 249–267?

EXAMINER'S NOTES, 2.1

4 Performance

Conflicts between characters (and within characters) are the basis for dramatic interest on stage. They can be used to make an audience laugh or to make an audience feel sympathy or to make an audience think about conflicts in life beyond the stage.

12 What advice would you give to the actors playing Oberon and Titania if you wanted one of them to seem more in control than the other in lines 60–145?

13 What advice would you give to the actor playing Helena if you wanted this part of the play to make the audience laugh (lines 188–244)?

14 What advice would you give to the actor playing Helena if you wanted the audience to pity her in lines 188–244?

5 Contexts and responses

Sometimes Shakespeare creates a setting that is familiar to his audience (e.g. a wood), and sometimes he creates a setting that is unfamiliar (e.g. Athens). These settings provide contexts that contrast the orderly, formal and sophisticated world of the Duke (Act 1 Scene 1) and the exotic, magical world of the wood. Some contexts can be suggested by the use of props and simple scenery (e.g. the wood); others are made believable by details of language (e.g. India). Most of the time, Shakespeare relies on language, not props and scenery, to create a believable context within the play.

15 What details of description does Shakespeare use to make the magical world of the wood seem a believable setting in lines 2–15, 249–256?

16 How do the details of Titania's description of India in lines 122–134 make it seem a believable setting?

17 Which of the attitudes, feelings and situations presented in this scene can be seen as particular to the context within the play and which can be seen as relevant to the context of people's lives today?

6 Reflecting on the scene

18 What similarities do you notice in Shakespeare's presentation of motives and relationships in the supernatural characters and the human characters in the scene?

19 Show how Shakespeare's use of language is effective in conveying both a sense of natural beauty and a sense of natural ugliness.

20 In what ways has your response to this scene been influenced by performance on stage, on screen or in the classroom?

EXAMINER'S TIP

Writing about drama

An audience watching a play must be gripped by what happens on stage, without reading the script.

Writing about a drama text needs to show how the plot is constructed to keep an audience interested, with shifts of scene and changes of character on stage. For example, switching between Oberon and Titania and the mortal lovers provides contrast but also keeps the theme of lovers' quarrels in the audience's mind.

EXAMINER'S TIP

Reflecting on the scene

Make sure you consider Shakespeare's skill in characterisation – as a writer making characters *seem* real in performance on stage.

This will help you treat them as imaginary characters created by Shakespeare to represent important themes, ideas and attitudes, rather than treating them as real people.

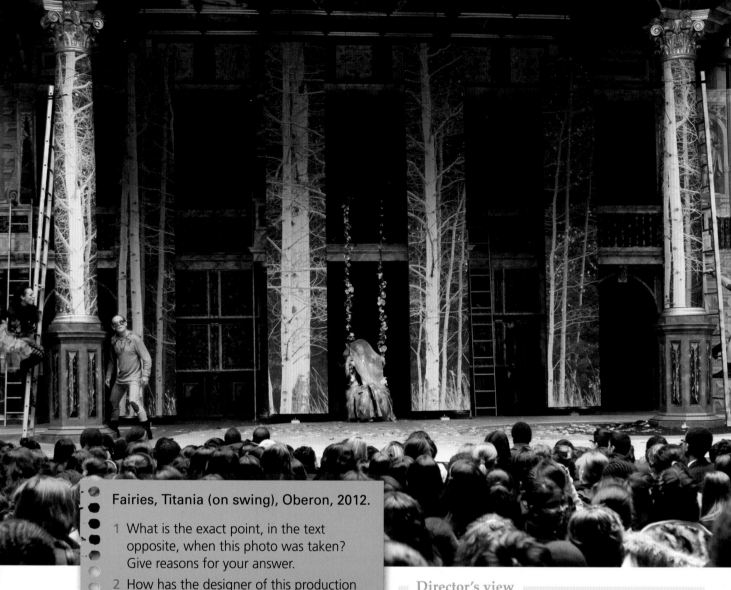

Fairies, Titania (on swing), Oberon, 2012.

1 What is the exact point, in the text opposite, when this photo was taken? Give reasons for your answer.

2 How has the designer of this production made the world of the wood look?

l–r Carlyss Peer, William Oxborrow, Emma Pallant, Chook Sibtain, Richard James-Neale

Actor's view

Carlyss Peer
A Fairy (and Helena), 2012

Playing a mythical creature you don't have the same restrictions that you have when you playing a normal human being. You can do anything you like. We thought, as a group, that the Fairies don't age in the same way that humans do, so that they're a bit more worldly, and in our production my Fairy was a bit more street. She had more of a London accent as opposed to Helena who was quite well spoken. It's the same as someone who grows up in a city, often they're quite worldly in a way different to people who grow up in a tiny village because they're exposed to a lot and there's a lot of fun to be had. So, I think that my Fairy knows a lot about the world and travels around a lot, which came through in the accent and the groundedness of the character. It was really fun to play. Our Fairies are quite mischievous. They like listening to people's conversations and wreaking havoc. Puck in particular is quite a naughty thing.

Director's view

Giles Block
Shakespeare's Globe text consultant

The play has more rhymed lines than any other Shakespeare play. Almost half the lines rhyme. We don't focus on these rhyming words as such; what we hear just seems right. Rhymes often end a scene; the right word comes at the right place as a sort of conclusion. Also, rhyme is clever. If you can rhyme with someone else, you're outwitting them.

The text on page 39 doesn't begin in rhyme, but it is in iambic pentameter, which Shakespeare used for most unrhymed speech. This has an important underlying rhythm which carries with it the sound of our heartbeat.

Titania's speech is followed by a song – one of the many ways that Shakespeare used rhyme, but far from the only way. The song is followed by a magic spell. Most magic spells rhyme, they seem to need to for the spell to work. Rhyme is a kind of magic. When two unconnected words make a rhyming connection, it seems to give an added meaning to what is said. The lines of the spell are shorter than iambic pentameter and it sound somehow unearthly.

Finally, Lysander speaks in rhyme. In this play, and other Shakespeare plays, lovers often speak in rhyme, maybe because they want everything to be harmonious and intimate. Rhyming words, which almost seem to kiss each other, seem intimate.

ACT 2 SCENE 2

Enter Titania and her attendant Fairies.

Titania   Come, now a roundel and a fairy song.
Then, for the third part of a minute, hence,
Some to kill cankers in the musk rose buds,
Some war with rere-mice for their leathern wings,
To make my small elves coats, and some keep back   5
The clamorous owl that nightly hoots and wonders
At our quaint spirits. Sing me now asleep,
Then to your offices, and let me rest.

[She lies down, the Fairies sing.]

All   You spotted snakes with double tongue,
Thorny hedgehogs be not seen;   10
Newts and blind-worms do no wrong,
Come not near our Fairy Queen.
Philomel, with melody,
Sing in our sweet lullaby.
Lulla lulla lullaby, lulla lulla lullaby,   15
Never harm, nor spell nor charm,
Come our lovely lady nigh;
So, good night, with lullaby.

First Fairy   Weaving spiders, come not here.
Hence, you long-legg'd spinners, hence.   20
Beetles black, approach not near,
Worm nor snail, do no offence.
Philomel, with melody
Sing in our sweet lullaby.
Lulla lulla lullaby, lulla lulla lullaby,   25
Never harm, nor spell nor charm,
Come our lovely lady nigh;
So, good night, with lullaby.   *Titania sleeps.*

Second Fairy   Hence away, now all is well.
One aloof stand sentinel.   *[Exit the Fairies.]* 30

Enter Oberon.
[He squeezing the juice of the flower in Titania's eyes.]

Oberon   What thou seest when thou dost wake,
Do it for thy true-love take.
Love and languish for his sake.
Be it ounce, or cat, or bear,
Pard, or boar with bristled hair,   35
In thy eye that shall appear
When thou wak'st, it is thy dear.
Wake when some vile thing is near.   *[Exit Oberon.]*

Enter Lysander and Hermia.

Lysander   Fair love, you faint with wand'ring in the wood,
And to speak troth, I have forgot our way.   40
We'll rest us Hermia, if you think it good,
And tarry for the comfort of the day.

---

1 **roundel:** dance in a circle

3 **cankers:** plant-eating caterpillars
4 **rere-mice:** bats
4 **leathern:** leather-like

6 **clamorous:** noisy
7 **quaint:** small, odd, delicate
8 **offices:** jobs

9 **double:** forked

11 **blind-worms:** adders

13 **Philomel:** the nightingale

17 **nigh:** near

20 **Hence:** go away

22 **offence:** harm

30 **aloof:** a little way away
30 **stand sentinel:** keep guard

33 **languish:** pine away
34 **ounce:** lynx
35 **Pard:** leopard

40 **to speak troth:** to tell you the truth
41 **think it good:** agree
42 **tarry:** wait
42 **comfort of the day:** encouragement of daylight

A

Louise Collins
Hermia, 2012

In our version I am exhausted, so we both decide that we will rest here. And then he decides that he wants to sleep near me. Even though I am completely in love with him, I am still virtuous and want to do things the right way. So she demands he 'lie further off'.

I have a suitcase, sleeping bag, a toilet bag. Inside my toilet bag I have face wipes, moisturiser, and an eye mask. I had my iPhone with my earphones, and I made a pillow out of my coat. It is really interesting because they are trying to work out who is boss and it is a bit of a game-playing scene, actually. It is full of fun, but it shows their love for each other.

I think it is very important scene. I, at least, have a lot of fun in this scene. The two of them, it is very exciting. They have run away, it is all working out, even though they are a bit lost, they are going to have a rest, and then it will all work out in the morning. It is really important, before Puck gets involved, that the two of them are having a really lovely time. There is a little bit of a quarrel, but it is fun.

Hermia and Lysander, 2012.

Photo A was taken during an evening performance, and Photos B and C during an afternoon performance. Ignore this fact and answer the questions assuming they were all taken at the same performance.

1 These photos were taken between lines 39 and 70. What is the correct order for the photos? Give reasons for your answer.

2 In Photo B, Lysander is looking at his mobile phone. Why might he be doing this? Quote from the play to support your answer.

Louise Collins, Peter Bray

Peter Bray
Lysander, 2012

Lysander's a huge romantic. The only things that he's brought with him on this running away trip are a heart-shaped helium balloon, a guitar, and a notebook of poems and love letters to Hermia. That's his plan, that's his preparation. And his iPhone, which runs out of signal immediately they get into the wood, and they get hopelessly lost.

B

C

Hermia	Be it so Lysander. Find you out a bed,
	For I upon this bank will rest my head.

43 **Find you out:** find yourself

Lysander	One turf shall serve as pillow for us both,	45
	One heart, one bed, two bosoms, and one troth.	

46 **bosoms:** hearts
46 **troth:** faithful promise of love

Hermia	Nay, good Lysander, for my sake, my dear,
	Lie further off yet, do not lie so near.

Lysander	O, take the sense, sweet, of my innocence.	
	Love takes the meaning in love's conference.	50
	I mean that my heart unto yours is knit,	
	So that but one heart we can make of it.	
	Two bosoms interchainèd with an oath,	
	So then two bosoms and a single troth.	
	Then by your side no bed-room me deny,	55
	For lying so, Hermia, I do not lie.	

49 **take the sense:** understand
50 **Love takes the meaning … conference:** lovers instinctively understand each other

56 **lie:** mislead you (pun on lying down)
57 **prettily:** cleverly, neatly
58 **much beshrew:** shame on

Hermia	Lysander riddles very prettily.	
	Now much beshrew my manners and my pride,	
	If Hermia meant to say Lysander lied.	
	But, gentle friend, for love and courtesy	60
	Lie further off, in human modesty.	
	Such separation, as may well be said	
	Becomes a virtuous bachelor and a maid,	
	So far be distant, and, good night, sweet friend.	
	Thy love ne'er alter till thy sweet life end.	65

63 **Becomes:** is suitable between
64 **So far be distant:** that's about the right distance

Lysander	Amen, amen, to that fair prayer, say I,
	And then end life when I end loyalty!
	Here is my bed, sleep give thee all his rest.

67 **And then end life … loyalty:** may I die if I'm ever disloyal to you

Hermia	With half that wish the wisher's eyes be pressed!

69 **With half that wish … be pressed!:** rather than all of sleep's rest, I'll take half – the rest goes to you

They sleep.
Enter Puck.

Puck	Through the forest have I gone,	70
	But Athenian found I none,	
	On whose eyes I might approve	
	This flower's force in stirring love.	
	Night and silence. — Who is here?	
	Weeds of Athens he doth wear.	75
	This is he, my master said,	
	Despisèd the Athenian maid.	
	And here the maiden, sleeping sound,	
	On the dank and dirty ground.	
	Pretty soul, she durst not lie	80
	Near this lack-love, this kill-courtesy.	

72 **approve:** test

75 **Weeds:** clothes

79 **dank:** damp
80 **durst not:** doesn't dare

[Squeezing the juice of the flower on Lysander's eyes.]

	Churl, upon thy eyes I throw	
	All the power this charm doth owe.	
	When thou wak'st, let love forbid	
	Sleep his seat on thy eyelid.	85
	So awake when I am gone,	
	For I must now to Oberon.	*Exit Puck.*

82 **Churl:** ill-mannered villain

83 **owe:** possess

84–5 **let love forbid … eyelid:** you'll be so in love you can't sleep

Enter Demetrius running, chased by Helena.

Lysander and Helena, 2012.

In this production:

- Lysander took off his shirt and t-shirt in an attempt to be more attractive to Helena
- Helena throws the t-shirt back at him
- the director cut Helena's speech in lines 127–136 to only four lines.

Carlyss Peer, Peter Bray

1 Explain which four lines you would keep.

2 On which line would you have Helena throw the t-shirt back at Lysander? Quote from the text to support your answer.

FROM THE REHEARSAL ROOM...

WHO LOVES WHO?

- Read the speeches of Lysander and Helena from lines 107–132, and Hermia in lines 149–160.
- What has changed, and what has stayed the same?

1 Copy the diagram below, and draw arrows to show who loves who. Use a different colour to show love as a result of the drug.

> After Puck drugs Lysander (2.2)

Hermia	Helena

Lysander	Demetrius

FROM THE REHEARSAL ROOM...

DRUGWATCH

This is a role-play. Use the instructions on page 34. In groups, cast the Investigator, Puck, Lysander, and the Observers.

- Puck should study lines 70–87, and Lysander lines 107–126.

1 Who drugged who?

2 What effect did the drug have?

Actor's view

Peter Bray
Lysander, 2012

On waking, it was an explosion of desire that was all poured forth into this one person, Helena. So for Lysander to wake up entirely in love with Helena, the worst thing that could happen, is that she simply doesn't believe him. He's in floods of tears because it's so frustrating. The desire for her won't let up, this potion is coursing round his veins. All he can think of is Helena and he has made literally no progress whatsoever.

Helena	Stay, though thou kill me, sweet Demetrius.
Demetrius	I charge thee, hence, and do not haunt me thus.
Helena	O wilt thou darkling leave me? Do not so.
Demetrius	Stay, on thy peril, I alone will go. *Exit Demetrius.*

89 charge thee: command you
89 haunt: follow me everywhere
90 **90 darkling:** in the dark

Helena
O, I am out of breath in this fond chase!
The more my prayer, the lesser is my grace.
Happy is Hermia, wheresoe'er she lies,
For she hath blessèd and attractive eyes.   95
How came her eyes so bright? Not with salt tears.
If so, my eyes are oftener washed than hers.
No, no, I am as ugly as a bear,
For beasts that meet me run away for fear:
Therefore no marvel though Demetrius   100
Do, as a monster, fly my presence thus.
What wicked and dissembling glass of mine
Made me compare with Hermia's sphery eyne? —
But who is here? Lysander on the ground?
Dead or asleep? I see no blood, no wound.   105
Lysander, if you live, good sir awake.

92 **fond:** double meaning: 1) infatuated; 2) foolish
93 **The more my prayer ... my grace:** the more I beg, the less I get
94 **wheresoe'er:** wherever

100 **Therefore no marvel though:** so it's no surprise that
101 **as a monster:** as if I was a monster
102 **dissembling:** deceiving
102 **glass:** mirror
103 **sphery eyne:** heavenly eyes

Lysander
[Waking.]   And run through fire I will for thy sweet sake.
Transparent Helena! Nature shows art,
That through thy bosom makes me see thy heart.
Where is Demetrius? O how fit a word   110
Is that vile name to perish on my sword!

108 **Transparent:** clear, without deceit
108 **Nature shows art:** nature's very clever

Helena
Do not say so, Lysander. Say not so.
What though he love your Hermia? Lord, what though?
Yet Hermia still loves you. Then be content.

113 **Lord, what though?:** good God, what does it matter?

Lysander
Content with Hermia? No, I do repent
The tedious minutes I with her have spent.   115
Not Hermia, but Helena I love.
Who will not change a raven for a dove?
The will of man is by his reason swayed,
And reason says you are the worthier maid.   120
Things growing are not ripe until their season,
So I, being young, till now ripe not to reason.
And touching now the point of human skill,
Reason becomes the marshal to my will,
And leads me to your eyes, where I o'erlook   125
Love's stories written in love's richest book.

118 **Who will not change ... a dove?:** Hermia is referred to as having a dark complexion (raven), Helena a pale one (dove)
119 **The will of man:** man's desires
122 **ripe not to reason:** was not old enough to see reason
123 **touching now the point of human skill:** now I'm mature enough
124 **becomes the marshal to:** can control
125 **o'erlook:** can read

Helena
Wherefore was I to this keen mockery born?
When, at your hands, did I deserve this scorn?
Is't not enough, is't not enough, young man,
That I did never, no nor never can,   130
Deserve a sweet look from Demetrius' eye,
But you must flout my insufficiency?
Good troth, you do me wrong, good sooth, you do,
In such disdainful manner me to woo.
But fare you well. Perforce I must confess   135
I thought you lord of more true gentleness.

127 **Wherefore:** why
127 **keen:** cruel
129 **Is't not:** isn't it

132 **flout my insufficiency:** mock my flaws
133 **Good troth:** truly
133 **good sooth:** indeed
135 **Perforce I must confess:** though I must say
136 **lord of more true gentleness:** more of a gentleman

A

B

Hermia: *A* 2008; *B* 2012.

1 These photos were taken three lines apart in the different productions. What are the main similarities and differences?

2 Read lines 149–160. Pick a line, or part of a line, to use as a caption for each photograph, and explain the reasons for your choices.

A Pippa Nixon, **B** Louise Collins

Director's Note, 2.2

✔ Titania falls asleep, and Oberon drugs her.

✔ Lysander and Hermia are tired and lost. They decide to sleep until daylight. Hermia makes Lysander sleep away from her.

✔ Puck sees them, assumes Lysander is the Athenian man he should drug, and drugs him.

✔ Demetrius and Helena enter. Demetrius leaves her alone in the wood.

✔ Helena wakes Lysander, who, because of the drug, falls madly in love with her. He tells her he loves her, but she assumes he is making fun of her. She leaves and he follows.

✔ Hermia wakes after a bad dream. She is scared, and cannot find Lysander. She goes to look for him.

SHAKESPEARE'S WORLD

The tiring house

In this scene, the Mechanicals have found a spot in the wood to rehearse their play. They imagine it to be just like an Elizabethan theatre with a *stage* and a *tiring house*. The tiring house is the area behind the stage, which nowadays we call the 'backstage'. It was where the actors would wait or 'retire' to hear their cues before going on stage. It was also where they would get dressed into their costumes (their *attire*). Props and costumes belonging to the company would have been stored in the tiring house and so would instruments and a range of other backstage items, such as makeup, wigs and fake beards.

Outlines of what happens in the play, called *plots*, were fixed to the wall inside the tiring house, so that actors knew where they had to be for each scene. The other side of the tiring house wall (the side the audience could see), called the *frons scenae*, was elaborately painted and decorated (see page 3). In this scene, Shakespeare asks his audience to use their imagination on two levels. The play is being performed on an actual stage, which the audience has to pretend is a 'green plot' and then re-imagine as a stage. At the same time we are asked to pretend the tiring house is a 'hawthorn brake' and then a tiring house again.

| | O, that a lady of one man refused, | |
| | Should of another therefore be abused! *Exit Helena.* | |

Lysander She sees not Hermia. Hermia, sleep thou there,
And never mayst thou come Lysander near. 140
For as a surfeit of the sweetest things
The deepest loathing to the stomach brings,
Or as the heresies that men do leave
Are hated most of those they did deceive,
So thou, my surfeit and my heresy, 145
Of all be hated, but the most of me!
And, all my powers, address your love and might,
To honour Helen, and to be her knight. *Exit Lysander.*

Hermia *[Waking.]* Help me, Lysander, help me! Do thy best
To pluck this crawling serpent from my breast. 150
Ay me, for pity! What a dream was here!
Lysander, look how I do quake with fear.
Methought a serpent eat my heart away,
And you sat smiling at his cruel prey.
Lysander! What, removed? Lysander, lord! 155
What, out of hearing? Gone? No sound, no word?
Alack, where are you? Speak, an if you hear.
Speak, of all loves! I swoon almost with fear.
No? then I well perceive you are not nigh.
Either death or you I'll find immediately. 160

Exit Hermia.

ACT 3 SCENE 1

Titania remains on the stage asleep. Enter the clowns –
Quince, Bottom, Flute, Snout, Snug, and Starveling.

Bottom Are we all met?

Quince Pat, pat. And here's a marvellous convenient place for
our rehearsal. This green plot shall be our stage, this
hawthorn-brake our tiring house, and we will do it in
action as we will do it before the Duke. 5

Bottom Peter Quince?

Quince What sayest thou, bully Bottom?

Bottom There are things in this comedy of Pyramus and Thisbe
that will never please. First, Pyramus must draw a
sword to kill himself, which the ladies cannot abide. 10
How answer you that?

Snout By'r lakin, a parlous fear.

Starveling I believe we must leave the killing out, when all is
done.

Bottom Not a whit, I have a device to make all well. Write me a 15
prologue, and let the prologue seem to say, we will do
no harm with our swords, and that Pyramus is not
killed indeed. And, for the more better assurance, tell

Glossary (right column):

137 **of:** by
138 **abused:** mistreated

141 **a surfeit:** too much of
143-4 **the heresies ... they did deceive:** false beliefs are most hated by those that once believed them

151 **Ay me, for pity!:** how dreadful!
151 **was here:** I have had
153 **Methought:** I imagined
153 **eat:** ate
154 **prey:** attack on me
155 **removed:** gone
157 **an if you hear:** if you can hear me
158 **of all loves:** for love's sake
158 **swoon:** faint
159 **I well perceive:** I can see

2 **Pat, pat:** right on time

4 **hawthorn-brake:** clump of hawthorn bushes
4 **tiring house:** actors' dressing room behind the stage

7 **bully:** a term of endearment used almost as if it were a title, me old mate

12 **By'r lakin:** short for 'By Our Lady-kin' (the Virgin Mary), a mild oath
12 **parlous:** perilous

15 **Not a whit:** not a bit of it
15 **device:** plan
16 **prologue:** speech to start the play
18 **for the more better assurance:** to be on the safe side

	them that I, Pyramus, am not Pyramus, but Bottom the weaver. This will put them out of fear. 20
Quince	Well, we will have such a prologue, and it shall be written in eight and six.
Bottom	No, make it two more, let it be written in eight and eight.
Snout	Will not the ladies be afeard of the lion?
Starveling	I fear it, I promise you. 25
Bottom	Masters, you ought to consider with yourself. To bring in (God shield us) a lion among ladies, is a most dreadful thing. For there is not a more fearful wild-fowl than your lion living, and we ought to look to 't.
Snout	Therefore another prologue must tell he is not a lion. 30
Bottom	Nay, you must name his name, and half his face must be seen through the lion's neck, and he himself must speak through, saying thus, or to the same defect: "Ladies," or "Fair-ladies, I would wish you," or "I would request you," or "I would entreat you not to fear, not 35 tremble. My life for yours. If you think I come hither as a lion, it were pity of my life. No, I am no such thing, I am a man as other men are." And there indeed let him name his name, and tell them plainly he is Snug the joiner. 40
Quince	Well, it shall be so. But there is two hard things. That is, to bring the moonlight into a chamber, for, you know, Pyramus and Thisbe meet by moonlight —
Snout	Doth the moon shine that night we play our play?
Bottom	A calendar, a calendar! Look in the almanac. Find out 45 moonshine, find out moonshine.
Quince	*[Looking at a book.]* Yes, it doth shine that night.
Bottom	Why, then may you leave a casement of the great chamber window (where we play) open, and the moon may shine in at the casement. 50
Quince	Ay, or else one must come in with a bush of thorns and a lantern, and say he comes to disfigure, or to present, the person of Moonshine. Then, there is another thing, we must have a wall in the great chamber; for Pyramus and Thisbe (says the story) did talk through the chink 55 of a wall.
Snout	You can never bring in a wall. What say you, Bottom?
Bottom	Some man or other must present Wall, and let him have some plaster, or some loam, or some roughcast about him, to signify wall. And let him hold his fingers thus, 60 and through that cranny shall Pyramus and Thisbe whisper.
Quince	If that may be, then all is well. Come, sit down, every mother's son, and rehearse your parts. Pyramus, you

22 **in eight and six:** alternating lines of eight and six syllables (usual in ballads)

28 **wild-fowl:** he means wild beast
29 **look to 't:** sort it out

33 **defect:** he means 'effect'

36 **My life for yours:** upon my life (literally: I'd die to save your life)
36 **hither:** here
37 **it were pity of my life:** double meaning: 1) I'd feel terrible; 2) my life would be in danger

45 **almanac:** calendar

48 **casement:** part of a window

51-2 **bush of thorns and a lantern:** said to be carried by the man in the moon
52 **disfigure:** he means 'figure' – represent

58 **present:** take the part of
59 **loam:** clay
59 **roughcast:** a mix of lime, gravel and water used to plaster the outside of walls
60 **thus:** like this
61 **cranny:** hole, split
63 **If that may be:** if we can do that
64 **rehearse:** speak

A

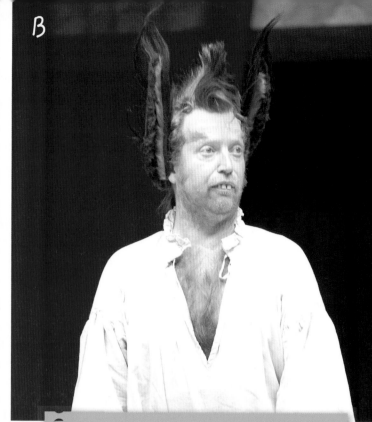

B

C

Bottom: *A* 2002; *B* 2008; *C* 2012.

Bottom reappears transformed. Later Puck tells Oberon he had given Bottom the head of an ass. This presents a problem for different productions. How realistically will they stage it?

1 The 2002 production had a dream theme and all the props and costumes came from the bedroom or bathroom. What is their solution?

2 What are the strengths and weaknesses of the three solutions here?

3 Which do you prefer and why?

A John Ramm; *B* Paul Hunter; *C* Russell Layton

SHAKESPEARE'S WORLD

'You speak all your part at once, cues and all.'

Flute is struggling to perform as 'Thisbe' from his *cue script* (see page 24). He has learnt it all, both his own lines, and his cues from the ends of Pyramus's speeches. But he does not understand how he should use it.

First, he misses his cue, and has to check it is his turn to speak. When he does begin, he simply says all his lines, without pausing between speeches to allow Pyramus to re-enter and to reply to him. Also, both actors find pronouncing certain words difficult – Bottom says 'odious' for 'odourous', whilst Flute misreads 'Ninus's' as 'Ninny's'.

	begin. When you have spoken your speech, enter into that brake, and so every one according to his cue.	65

Enter Puck, unseen by the others on stage.

Puck   [*Aside.*] What hempen homespuns have we swagg'ring here,
So near the cradle of the Fairy Queen?
What, a play toward? I'll be an auditor,
An actor too perhaps, if I see cause.   70

Quince   Speak, Pyramus. Thisbe stand forth.

Pyramus (Bottom)   *Thisbe, the flowers of odious savours sweet, —*

Quince   *Odours, odorous.*

Pyramus (Bottom)   *odours savours sweet,*
So hath thy breath, my dearest Thisbe dear.
But hark, a voice. Stay thou but here awhile,   75
And by and by I will to thee appear.   *Exit Bottom.*

Puck   A stranger Pyramus than e'er played here.   [*Exit.*]

Flute   Must I speak now?

Quince   Ay, marry, must you. For you must understand he goes
but to see a noise that he heard, and is to come again.   80

Thisbe (Flute)   *Most radiant Pyramus, most lily-white of hue,*
Of colour like the red rose on triumphant briar,
Most brisky juvenal, and eke most lovely Jew,
As true as truest horse, that yet would never tire,
I'll meet thee, Pyramus, at Ninny's tomb.   85

Quince   "Ninus' tomb," man! Why, you must not speak that yet.
That you answer to Pyramus. You speak all your part at
once, cues and all. Pyramus enter, your cue is past, it is,
"never tire."

Flute   O!   90

Thisbe (Flute)   *As true as truest horse, that yet would never tire,*

[Enter Puck, and Bottom with an ass's head.]

Pyramus (Bottom)   *If I were fair, Thisbe, I were only thine.*

Quince   O monstrous! O strange! We are haunted. Pray, masters,
fly, masters! Help!

Quince, Bottom, Flute, Snout, Snug, and Starveling run off stage in different directions.

Puck   I'll follow you. I'll lead you about a round,   95
Through bog, through bush, through brake, through briar.
Sometime a horse I'll be, sometime a hound,
A hog, a headless bear, sometime a fire,
And neigh, and bark, and grunt, and roar, and burn,
Like horse, hound, hog, bear, fire, at every turn.   100

Exit Puck. Enter Bottom with an ass's head.

---

66 **brake:** clump of bushes
66 **and so every one:** and you all do that
67 **hempen homespuns:** stupid peasants (hemp made a scratchy cloth, which only the poor wore)
68 **cradle:** resting place
69 **toward:** being prepared
69 **I'll be an auditor:** I'll listen

72 *odious:* hateful; he means 'odours' – smells
72 *savours:* smells

76 *by and by:* soon

77 **e'er:** ever

79 **marry:** 'by the Virgin Mary', used at the start of a sentence for emphasis as 'well' is now
79–80 **he goes but:** he's only going to
81 *hue:* colour
83 *brisky juvenal:* energetic young man
83 *eke:* also
83 *Jew:* desperate rhyme with 'hue'
85 *Ninny's:* fool; he means 'Ninus' an ancient king

92 *fair:* handsome

95 **a round:** a circular dance

98 **fire:** dancing light that, in the marshes, led travellers astray

A

B

C

Titania and Bottom: *A* 2002; *B* 2008; *C* 2012.

1 Study lines 122–144 in the text. Who is doing the running in this relationship? Quote from the text to support your answer.

2 How well is this shown in:

a) the 2002 production? (A)

b) the 2008 production? (B)

c) the 2012 production? (C)

A Geraldine Alexander, John Ramm

B Siobhan Redmond, Paul Hunter

C Russell Layton, Emma Pallant

Bottom	Why do they run away? This is a knavery of them to make me afeard.

Enter Snout.

Snout	O Bottom, thou art changed. What do I see on thee?
Bottom	What do you see? You see an ass-head of your own, do you?

Exit Snout. Enter Quince.

Quince	Bless thee, Bottom, bless thee. Thou art translated.

Exit Quince.

Bottom	I see their knavery. This is to make an ass of me, to fright me, if they could. But I will not stir from this place, do what they can. I will walk up and down here, and I will sing, that they shall hear I am not afraid.
	[Sings.] The ousel cock so black of hue,
	With orange-tawny bill.
	The throstle with his note so true,
	The wren with little quill,—
Titania	What angel wakes me from my flowery bed?
Bottom	The finch, the sparrow and the lark,
	The plain-song cuckoo gray,
	Whose note full many a man doth mark,
	And dares not answer nay —
	For indeed, who would set his wit to so foolish a bird? Who would give a bird the lie, though he cry "cuckoo" never so?
Titania	I pray thee, gentle mortal, sing again,
	Mine ear is much enamoured of thy note.
	So is mine eye enthrallèd to thy shape,
	And thy fair virtue's force (perforce) doth move me
	On the first view to say, to swear, I love thee.
Bottom	Methinks mistress, you should have little reason for that. And yet, to say the truth, reason and love keep little company together now-a-days. The more the pity that some honest neighbours will not make them friends. Nay, I can gleek upon occasion.
Titania	Thou art as wise as thou art beautiful.
Bottom	Not so neither. But if I had wit enough to get out of this wood, I have enough to serve mine own turn.
Titania	Out of this wood do not desire to go,
	Thou shalt remain here, whether thou wilt or no.
	I am a spirit of no common rate.
	The summer still doth tend upon my state,
	And I do love thee. Therefore go with me.
	I'll give thee fairies to attend on thee,
	And they shall fetch thee jewels from the deep,
	And sing, while thou on pressèd flowers dost sleep.
	And I will purge thy mortal grossness so

105

110

115

120

125

130

135

140

101 a knavery of them: a trick of theirs

105 translated: changed into something else

108 do what they can: no matter what they do
110 ousel cock: male blackbird
111 bill: beak
112 throstle: thrush
113 little quill: high, sharp, song

116 plain-song cuckoo: cuckoo with his simple song (that sounds like 'cuckold', a man whose wife has been unfaithful)
117 mark: hear, notice
118 And dares not answer nay: and can't deny (that he is a cuckold)
120 give a bird the lie: accuse a bird of lying
121 never so: ever so much
123 of thy note: by your singing
124 So: in the same way
124 enthrallèd to: bewitched by
125 thy fair virtue's force: the power of your qualities
125 (perforce) doth move me: forces me

131 gleek: joke

134 to serve mine own turn: for me

136 wilt: want to
137 common rate: ordinary sort
138 tend: attend, wait upon

141 the deep: the bottom of the sea
143 purge: purify
143 thy mortal grossness: the clumsiness of your human body

Bottom (in the chair) attended by Peaseblossom, Cobweb, Moth, and Mustardseed, 2012.

Usually, in productions of *A Midsummer Night's Dream*, the Fairies are dressed in colours which blend in with the wood (see page 38). These Fairies are very different. Using the key to the right, which is which? Give reasons for your answers.

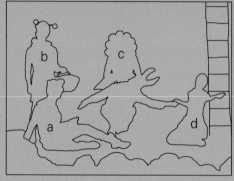

FROM THE REHEARSAL ROOM...

DRUGWATCH

This is a role-play. Use the instructions on page 34. In groups, cast the Investigator, Oberon, Moth, and the Observers.

- Oberon should study Act 2 Scene 2, lines 32–38; Moth the text on page 53.

1 Who drugged who?

2 How does Titania behave after she has been drugged?

3 Is Oberon happy with the way the plan is working?

Director's Note, 3.1

✔ The Mechanicals rehearse their play.

✔ To have some fun, Puck changes Bottom's head to an ass's head while Bottom is offstage.

✔ Bottom re-enters and the Mechanicals run away, scared of the monster he has become.

✔ Bottom wakes Titania, who, because of the drug, falls madly in love with him.

✔ Titania makes her Fairies serve Bottom, then takes him off to her private resting place.

✔ What is going to happen next?

That thou shalt like an airy spirit go.
Peaseblossom, Cobweb, Moth, and Mustardseed!   145

Enter these four Fairies.

Peaseblossom Ready.

Cobweb   And I.

Moth   And I.

Mustardseed   Where shall we go?

Titania Be kind and courteous to this gentleman.
Hop in his walks and gambol in his eyes,
Feed him with apricocks and dewberries,
With purple grapes, green figs, and mulberries.   150
The honey-bags steal from the humble-bees,
And for night-tapers crop their waxen thighs
And light them at the fiery glow-worm's eyes,
To have my love to bed and to arise.
And pluck the wings from painted butterflies   155
To fan the moonbeams from his sleeping eyes.
Nod to him elves, and do him courtesies.

Peaseblossom Hail mortal.

Cobweb   Hail.

Moth   Hail.

Mustardseed   Hail.

Bottom I cry your worships mercy heartily. *[To Cobweb.]*
I beseech your worship's name.   160

Cobweb Cobweb.

Bottom I shall desire you of more acquaintance, good Master
Cobweb. If I cut my finger, I shall make bold with you.
— Your name, honest gentleman?

Peaseblossom Peaseblossom.   165

Bottom I pray you, commend me to Mistress Squash, your
mother, and to Master Peascod, your father. Good
Master Peaseblossom, I shall desire of you more
acquaintance too. — Your name, I beseech you, sir?

Mustardseed Mustardseed.   170

Bottom Good Master Mustardseed, I know your patience well.
That same cowardly, giant-like ox-beef hath devoured
many a gentleman of your house. I promise you, your
kindred had made my eyes water ere now. I desire your
more acquaintance, good Master Mustardseed.   175

Titania Come, wait upon him, lead him to my bower.
The moon methinks looks with a watery eye,
And when she weeps, weeps every little flower,
Lamenting some enforcèd chastity.
Tie up my love's tongue, bring him silently.   180

She exits, the Fairies bring Bottom after her.

148 **in his eyes:** for him to see
149 **apricocks:** apricots
149 **dewberries:** blackberries

151 **humble-bees:** bumble-bees
152 **night-tapers:** candles
152 **crop their waxen thighs:** collect
their beeswax

157 **do him courtesies:** greet him
politely

159 **I cry your worships mercy:** he
means to use a formal greeting,
but begs pardon
160 **beseech:** ask

163 **If I cut my finger:** cobwebs
were used to stop small cuts
bleeding

171 **your patience:** how well you put
up with things
172-3 **hath devoured ... of your
house:** mustard was often eaten
with beef
174 **kindred:** family
174 **made my eyes water:** mustard
is hot, like chilli
176 **bower:** resting place
179 **enforcèd chastity:** this could
either mean rape, (chastity being
forced), or being forced to be
chaste

Puck makes a spectacular entrance, 2012.

1 Puck appears to be sliding down a rope with one hand. This would be impossible. How has it been staged?

2 Why might the director have decided to stage Puck's entrance like this, rather than just have him walk onto the stage?

Fergal McElherron

Enter Oberon.

Oberon I wonder, if Titania be awaked,
Then what it was that next came in her eye,
Which she must dote on in extremity.

Enter Puck.

Here comes my messenger. How now, mad spirit?
What night-rule now about this haunted grove?   5

Puck My mistress with a monster is in love.
Near to her close and consecrated bower,
While she was in her dull and sleeping hour,
A crew of patches, rude mechanicals,
That work for bread upon Athenian stalls,   10
Were met together to rehearse a play
Intended for great Theseus' nuptial day.
The shallowest thick-skin of that barren sort,
Who Pyramus presented in their sport,
Forsook his scene and entered in a brake.   15
When I did him at this advantage take,
An ass's nole I fixèd on his head.
Anon his Thisbe must be answerèd,
And forth my mimic comes. When they him spy,
As wild geese that the creeping fowler eye,   20
Or russet-pated choughs, many in sort,
Rising and cawing at the gun's report,
Sever themselves and madly sweep the sky.
So, at his sight, away his fellows fly,
And at our stamp, here o'er and o'er one falls,   25
He "murder" cries, and help from Athens calls.
Their sense thus weak, lost with their fears thus strong,
Made senseless things begin to do them wrong.
For briars and thorns at their apparel snatch,
Some sleeves, some hats, from yielders all things catch.   30
I led them on in this distracted fear,
And left sweet Pyramus translated there.
When in that moment, so it came to pass,
Titania waked and straightway loved an ass.

Oberon This falls out better than I could devise.   35
But hast thou yet latched the Athenian's eyes
With the love juice, as I did bid thee do?

Puck I took him sleeping (that is finished too)
And the Athenian woman by his side,
That, when he waked, of force she must be eyed.   40

Enter Demetrius and Hermia.

Oberon Stand close. This is the same Athenian.

Puck This is the woman, but not this the man.

[They stand aside.]

Demetrius O why rebuke you him that loves you so?
Lay breath so bitter on your bitter foe.

2 **next came in her eye:** she saw next
3 **in extremity:** madly

5 **night-rule:** mischief done in the night

9 **patches:** fools
9 **rude mechanicals:** common workmen
10 **work for bread:** earn their living
13 **shallowest thick-skin:** stupidest and most insensitive person
13 **barren sort:** stupid lot
15 **Forsook:** left
15 **scene:** stage
16 **I did him at this advantage take:** I took this chance
17 **nole:** head
18 **Anon:** soon
19 **forth:** out
19 **mimic:** actor
20 **fowler:** wild bird hunter
20 **eye:** see
21 **russet-pated choughs:** a red-beaked crow with black feathers
21 **many in sort:** in a big flock
22 **report:** noise of a gun firing
23 **Sever themselves:** scatter
25 **at our stamp:** when I stamped

28 **senseless things:** inanimate objects
28 **do them wrong:** harm them
29 **apparel:** clothing
30 **yielders:** those giving things up
32 **translated:** changed into something else
33 **in that moment:** just then

35 **I could devise:** I could have planned
36 **latched:** covered

40 **of force she must be eyed:** she had to be the first thing he saw

41 **Stand close:** out of the way, hide

44 **Lay breath so bitter on your bitter foe:** save bitter words for your enemies

Actor's view

Louise Collins
Hermia, 2012

What I did is imagine that she has run around in the pitch dark looking for Lysander. Screaming, shouting, out of breath, crying. Tripped over branches – she's probably got scratches all over her hands and knees because she has stumbled so many times. And she discovers Demetrius, and I think, automatically, just thinks he has done it. There is no way Lysander would have left her. Demetrius has come along and killed him in his sleep. He could not even fight him awake, he is that much of a coward. So I think she feels frightened in his company, but also in absolute rage. So there are the two emotions fighting against one another – one, she wants to run away from him, two, she wants to attack him and know where Lysander is and what Demetrius has done. So it is a mixture of big emotions going on at the same time. She flips from rage to fear very quickly.

Hermia and Demetrius, (with Oberon and Puck on the pillars), 2008.

1 a) What do the following suggest about the relationship between Hermia and Demetrius at this point in the play?

   i) The body language of the actors.
   ii) Where the director has put the actors on the stage.

   b) How well does this fit with the text? Quote from the text to support your answer.

2 How has the director used the stage pillars?

l–r Tom Mannion, Pippa Nixon, Oliver Boot, Michael Jibson

Hermia	Now I but chide, but I should use thee worse,
	For thou, I fear, hast given me cause to curse.
	If thou hast slain Lysander in his sleep,
	Being o'er shoes in blood, plunge in the deep,
	And kill me too.
	The sun was not so true unto the day
	As he to me. Would he have stol'n away
	From sleeping Hermia? I'll believe as soon
	This whole earth may be bored, and that the moon
	May through the centre creep, and so displease
	Her brother's noontide with th' Antipodes.
	It cannot be but thou hast murdered him.
	So should a murderer look, so dead, so grim.
Demetrius	So should the murdered look, and so should I,
	Pierced through the heart with your stern cruelty.
	Yet you, the murderer, look as bright, as clear,
	As yonder Venus in her glimmering sphere.
Hermia	What's this to my Lysander? Where is he?
	Ah, good Demetrius, wilt thou give him me?
Demetrius	I'd rather give his carcass to my hounds.
Hermia	Out, dog! Out, cur! Thou driv'st me past the bounds
	Of maiden's patience. Hast thou slain him then?
	Henceforth be never numbered among men.
	O, once tell true. Tell true, e'en for my sake!
	Durst thou have looked upon him, being awake,
	And hast thou killed him sleeping? O brave touch!
	Could not a worm, an adder, do so much?
	An adder did it! For with doubler tongue
	Than thine (thou serpent) never adder stung.
Demetrius	You spend your passion on a misprised mood.
	I am not guilty of Lysander's blood.
	Nor is he dead for aught that I can tell.
Hermia	I pray thee tell me then that he is well.
Demetrius	And if I could, what should I get therefore?
Hermia	A privilege, never to see me more.
	And from thy hated presence part I so,
	See me no more, whether he be dead or no. *She exits.*
Demetrius	There is no following her in this fierce vein,
	Here therefore for a while I will remain.
	So sorrow's heaviness doth heavier grow
	For debt that bankrupt sleep doth sorrow owe,
	Which now in some slight measure it will pay,
	If for his tender here I make some stay.
	He lies down and sleeps.
Oberon	What hast thou done? Thou hast mistaken quite
	And laid the love juice on some true-love's sight.
	Of thy misprision must perforce ensue
	Some true-love turned, and not a false turned true.

Line numbers: 45, 50, 55, 60, 65, 70, 75, 80, 85, 90

Glossary:

45 **I but chide:** I'm only scolding you
45 **use thee worse:** be harder on you
48 **o'er:** over
50 **true unto:** faithful to
52 **I'll believe as soon:** it's as likely that
53 **bored:** drilled right through
54 **displease:** upset
55 **Her brother's:** the sun's
55 **with th' Antipodes:** on the other side of the world
56 **cannot be but:** must be
57 **dead:** pale
61 **Venus:** the planet, called 'the evening star'
61 **glimmering sphere:** shining orbit
62 **to:** got to do with
65 **cur:** dog
67 **be never numbered among men:** you don't count as a man
69 **Durst thou:** did you dare to
70 **O brave touch!:** well done!
71 **worm:** snake
72 **For with doubler tongue:** because no tongue could be more deceitful; also refers to a snake's forked tongue
74 **spend your passion ... mood:** are angry for no good reason
76 **for aught that I can tell:** as far as I know
78 **therefore:** for it
81 **no:** not
82 **vein:** mood
84–5 **So sorrow's ... doth sorrow owe:** I'm worn down by tiredness and sorrow
87 **If for his tender here I make some stay:** if I lie here a while and try to sleep
90 **Of thy misprision must perforce ensue:** the consequence of your mistake is bound to be

A

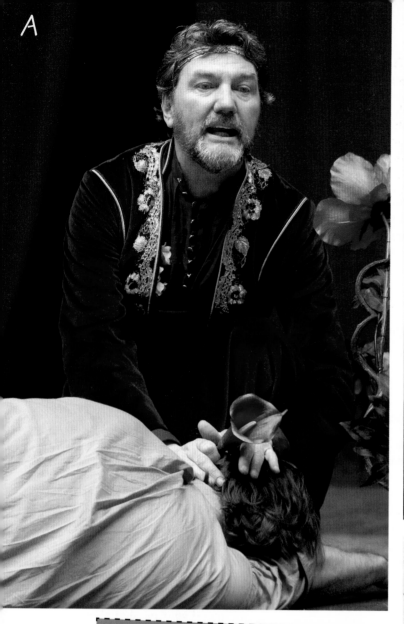

B

1 These two moments are very similar.
Does this mean the director of the 2008
production must have copied the director of
the 2002 production? Support your answer
with quotations from the text.

A Tom Mannion, Oliver Boot *B* Paul Higgins,
Keith Dunphy

Actor's view

Richard James-Neale
Demetrius, 2012

*In our production, Oberon and Puck both had
this ability that when they clicked their fingers
anything that they wanted to happen on the
stage, happened. So, the actual technique of
being drugged: Oberon would click his fingers and it forced the
sleepy Demetrius to become very rigid and sit bolt upright and
then the drug was administered into his eye, then Oberon very
casually clicked his fingers again and Demetrius fell asleep, very
limp again.*

FROM THE REHEARSAL ROOM...

STAGING THE DRUGGING

Oberon says of the love potion in Act 2 Scene 1:
The juice of it on sleeping eye-lids laid
Will make or man or woman madly dote
Upon the next live creature that it sees.

- As the director, how would you stage this?
  Consider these points plus ideas of your own.

  - The people administering the potion are
    fairies and can use magic.

  - Each individual might react differently to
    the potion when it's administered.

  - 'Streak', 'anoint' and 'throw' are some of
    the words used by Oberon and Puck when
    talking about or using the potion.

- Try staging your ideas.

1 Describe your best ideas.

Puck	Then fate o'er-rules, that one man holding troth,	
	A million fail, confounding oath on oath.	
Oberon	About the wood go swifter than the wind,	
	And Helena of Athens look thou find.	95
	All fancy-sick she is, and pale of cheer,	
	With sighs of love that costs the fresh blood dear.	
	By some illusion see thou bring her here.	
	I'll charm his eyes, against she do appear.	
Puck	I go, I go, look how I go,	100
	Swifter than arrow from the Tartar's bow.	

Exit Puck.

le dye,
chery,
eye.   *[Squeezing the flower*
oth espy,   *over Demetrius' eyes.]* 105
riously
sky.
if she be by,
dy.

Enter Puck.

band,   110
nd,
ook by me,
's fee.
pageant see?
se mortals be!   115

se they make
is to awake.

e woo one,
sport alone.
best please me   120
ously.

Lysander and Helena.

ık that I should woo in scorn?
ever come in tears.
veep, and vows so born,
ruth appears.   125
s in me seem scorn to you,
faith to prove them true?

Helena	You do advance your cunning more and more.	
	When truth kills truth, O devilish holy fray!	
	These vows are Hermia's. Will you give her o'er?	130
	Weigh oath with oath, and you will nothing weigh.	
	Your vows to her, and me, (put in two scales)	
	Will even weigh, and both as light as tales.	
Lysander	I had no judgment when to her I swore.	
Helena	Nor none, in my mind, now you give her o'er.	135

92 **o'er-rules:** dictates
92 **one man holding troth:** for every man that's faithful
93 **confounding oath on oath:** breaking promises of faithfulness over and over
95 **look thou:** make sure you
96 **fancy-sick:** lovesick
96 **cheer:** face
97 **sighs of love ... blood dear:** it was thought each sigh drained a drop of blood from the heart
98 **illusion:** trick
99 **against:** ready for when
101 **the Tartar's bow:** the Tartars of Central Asia were famous archers

104 **apple:** the pupil

109 **Beg of her for remedy:** you'll be pleading with her to love you

113 **fee:** payment
114 **fond pageant:** foolish show

119 **alone:** in itself

121 **befall prepost'rously:** have ridiculous consequences

122 **in scorn:** to mock you

124 **Look:** see how
125 **nativity:** birth
127 **the badge of faith:** the sign of true love
128 **advance:** increase
128 **cunning:** trickery
129 **truth kills truth:** a promise to one person cancels a promise to another
129 **devilish holy fray:** a conflict between true and false promises
130 **o'er:** up
133 **even weigh:** balance each other
133 **as light as tales:** as false as fairy stories

Working Cut – text for experiment

Lys	Why seek'st thou me? Could not this make thee know The hate I bear thee made me leave thee so?
Herm	You speak not as you think. It cannot be.
Hel	Lo, she is one of this confederacy, Injurious Hermia, most ungrateful maid, Have you conspired, have you with these contrived To bait me with this foul derision?
Herm	I am amazed at your passionate words. I scorn you not. It seems that you scorn me.
Hel	Have you not set Lysander, as in scorn, To follow me and praise my eyes and face? And made your other love, Demetrius, To call me goddess, nymph, divine and rare
Herm	I understand not what you mean by this.
Hel	Ay, do. Persever, counterfeit sad looks, Make mouths upon me when I turn my back, Wink each at other, hold the sweet jest up.
Lys	Helen, I love thee, by my life, I do.
Dem	I say I love thee more than he can do.
Lys	If thou say so, withdraw and prove it too
Dem	Quick, come!
Herm	Lysander, whereto tends all this?
Lys	Hang off thou cat, thou burr. Vile thing let loose, Or I will shake thee from me like a serpent.
Herm	Why are you grown so rude? What change is this Sweet love?
Lys	Thy love? Out, tawny Tartar, out! Out loathed medicine! O hated potion hence!
Herm	Do you not jest?
Hel	Yes sooth, and so do you.
Lys	What, should I hurt her, strike her, kill her dead? Although I hate her, I'll not harm her so.
Herm	What, can you do me greater harm than hate? Hate me? Wherefore? O me, what news, my love? Since night you loved me, yet since night you left me. In earnest, shall I say?
Lys	Ay, by my life, And never did desire to see thee more. Be certain, nothing truer; 'tis no jest That I do hate thee and love Helena.
Herm	O me! *[To Helena.]* You juggler, you canker-blossom, You thief of love! What, have you come by night And stolen my love's heart from him?
Hel	Fine, i'faith. Have you no modesty, no maiden shame, Fie, fie, you counterfeit. You puppet, you!
Herm	"Puppet"? Why so? Ay, that way goes the game. Now I perceive that she hath made compare Between our statures. She hath urged her height, And with her personage, her tall personage, Her height, forsooth, she hath prevailed with him.

FROM THE REHEARSAL ROOM...

LITTLE ARROWS

- As a group, read the *Working Cut* of the lovers' fight, taking a line each.
- Now allocate roles and read through again. At the end of each character's speech, use one word to describe how that character is feeling at that time.
- Who changes in their emotions and who stays the same? What is happening to make them change?
- As a group, discuss what advice you would give the actors playing Hermia and Lysander to show how their relationship has changed from the previous scene.
- Helena and Hermia have not been affected by the drug. How might they be feeling in comparison to Lysander and Demetrius?

	And are you grown so high in his esteem Because I am so dwarfish and so low? How low am I, thou painted maypole? Speak! How low am I? I am not yet so low But that my nails can reach unto thine eyes. *[She runs at Helena.]*
Hel	Let her not strike me. You perhaps may think, Because she is something lower than myself, That I can match her.
Herm	Lower? Hark again.
Lys	Be not afraid, she shall not harm thee Helena.
Dem	No, sir, she shall not, though you take her part.
Hel	O, when she is angry, she is keen and shrewd. She was a vixen when she went to school, And though she be but little, she is fierce.
Herm	"Little" again? Nothing but "low" and "little"? Let me come to her!
Lys	Get you gone, you dwarf; You minimus of hind'ring knot-grass made; You bead, you acorn.

Lysander   Demetrius loves her, and he loves not you.

Demetrius wakes up.

Demetrius   O Helen, goddess, nymph, perfect, divine,
To what, my love, shall I compare thine eyne?
Crystal is muddy. O how ripe in show
Thy lips, those kissing cherries, tempting grow!
That pure congealèd white, high Taurus snow,
Fanned with the eastern wind, turns to a crow
When thou hold'st up thy hand. O, let me kiss
This princess of pure white, this seal of bliss.

Helena   O spite! O hell! I see you all are bent
To set against me for your merriment.
If you were civil and knew courtesy,
You would not do me thus much injury.
Can you not hate me, as I know you do,
But you must join in souls to mock me too?
If you were men, as men you are in show,
You would not use a gentle lady so,
To vow, and swear, and superpraise my parts,
When I am sure you hate me with your hearts.
You both are rivals, and love Hermia,
And now both rivals to mock Helena.
A trim exploit, a manly enterprise,
To conjure tears up in a poor maid's eyes
With your derision. None of noble sort
Would so offend a virgin, and extort
A poor soul's patience, all to make you sport.

Lysander   You are unkind, Demetrius. Be not so.
For you love Hermia, this you know I know.
And here with all good will, with all my heart,
In Hermia's love I yield you up my part.
And yours of Helena to me bequeath,
Whom I do love, and will do till my death.

Helena   Never did mockers waste more idle breath.

Demetrius   Lysander, keep thy Hermia. I will none.
If e'er I loved her, all that love is gone.
My heart to her, but as guest-wise, sojourned,
And now to Helen is it home returned,
There to remain.

Lysander   Helena, it is not so.

Demetrius   Disparage not the faith thou dost not know,
Lest, to thy peril thou a-buy it dear.
Look, where thy love comes. Yonder is thy dear.

Enter Hermia.

Hermia   Dark night, that from the eye his function takes,
The ear more quick of apprehension makes,
Wherein it doth impair the seeing sense,
It pays the hearing double recompense.

---

138 **thine eyne:** your eyes

140

141 **congealèd:** frozen
141 **Taurus:** mountains in Turkey
142 **turns to a crow:** turns black as a crow
144 **princess of pure white:** her hand
145
144 **seal of:** promise of
145 **bent:** decided
146 **To set:** to work together
147 **were civil:** had any manners

150 150 **join in souls:** unite

152 **use:** treat
153 **parts:** qualities

155

157 **trim exploit:** neat plot
158 **conjure:** raise, as if by magic
159 **derision:** mockery
160 160 **extort:** torture
161 **all to make you sport:** just for a laugh

165

166 **to me bequeath:** give to me

169 **I will none:** I don't want her
170

171 **but as guest-wise, sojourned:** was just visiting her for a while

174 **Disparage not:** don't criticise
175 175 **a-buy it dear:** pay dearly for it

178 **more quick of apprehension:** sharper of hearing
179 **Wherein:** where
179 **impair:** restrict
180 180 **pays the hearing double recompense:** makes the hearing twice as sharp

61

GIVING STATUS

This activity uses a pack of playing cards. Remove the picture cards. Shuffle the remaining cards and each student takes one, face down. Students must not see their own card.

- The cards represent status, with A the lowest and 10 the highest.
- Hold your card on your forehead, face out, without looking at it.
- Mingle around the room reacting to each person individually according to the number on their card, and note how they react to you. For example you might bow to a 10 and dismiss an A.
- With the cards still on your forehead line up from left to right placing yourself in order of importance. 10s to the left and As to the right.
- Once the line has been made, look at your card, and see how accurate the line is.

1 Were you correct in your placing?
2 How did you know what status you were?
3 Which were the hardest to achieve?

TAKING STATUS

This time, the pack should only have pairs of cards (two As, two 10s, and so on). Shuffle the pack and hand out the cards individually. This time students can look at their own card.

- This time take on the status of your card. So, if you are a 10 you might want to stand upright and walk with extreme confidence.
- Mingle around the room saying only "I understand not what you mean by this", when you meet others, keeping to your given status.
- If you speak to anyone that you think has the same status as yourself, stay with them.
- When everyone has grouped up or found a partner, look at your cards and compare.

1 What made you choose your partner? What was it that you recognised?
2 Can you think of a moment where giving yourself a certain status might be useful?
- In small groups, read the first scene between Helena and Hermia (Act 1 Scene 1, lines 180–203).
3 What status number would you give to Helena and to Hermia in this scene? Support each answer with quotations from the text.
- Now read the *Working Cut* on page 60.
- In your groups discuss the difference in status between the girls in this scene and compare it to the one you have just read.
4 What status are Helena and Hermia now? Again, support your answer with quotations.
5 What changes in the scenes have contributed to the change in status of the characters?

Helena and Hermia, 2008.

This was taken during the speech where Helena rounds on Hermia (lines 192–219). Which line best fits the photo?

a) 'Lo, she is one of this confederacy'
b) 'For parting us. O, is it all forgot?'
c) 'It is not friendly, 'tis not maidenly.'

Laura Rogers, Pippa Nixon

Thou art not by mine eye, Lysander, found,
Mine ear, I thank it, brought me to thy sound.
But why unkindly didst thou leave me so?

Lysander   Why should he stay, whom love doth press to go?

184 press: urge

Hermia   What love could press Lysander from my side?   185

Lysander   Lysander's love (that would not let him bide)
Fair Helena, who more engilds the night
Than all yon fiery oes and eyes of light.
Why seek'st thou me? Could not this make thee know
The hate I bear thee made me leave thee so?   190

186 bide: stay
187 more engilds: glows more golden in
188 yon fiery oes and eyes of light: the stars

Hermia   You speak not as you think. It cannot be.

Helena   Lo, she is one of this confederacy,
Now I perceive they have conjoined all three
To fashion this false sport in spite of me. –
Injurious Hermia, most ungrateful maid,   195
Have you conspired, have you with these contrived
To bait me with this foul derision?
Is all the counsel that we two have shared,
The sisters' vows, the hours that we have spent,
When we have chid the hasty-footed time   200
For parting us. O, is it all forgot?
All school-days' friendship, childhood innocence?
We, Hermia, like two artificial gods,
Have with our needles created both one flower,
Both on one sampler, sitting on one cushion,   205
Both warbling of one song, both in one key,
As if our hands, our sides, voices, and minds
Had been incorporate. So we grew together,
Like to a double cherry, seeming parted,
But yet a union in partition,   210
Two lovely berries moulded on one stem,
So with two seeming bodies, but one heart,
Two of the first, like coats in heraldry,
Due but to one and crownèd with one crest.
And will you rent our ancient love asunder,   215
To join with men in scorning your poor friend?
It is not friendly, 'tis not maidenly.
Our sex, as well as I, may chide you for it,
Though I alone do feel the injury.

192 confederacy: conspiracy
193 conjoined: united
194 fashion: design
194 in spite of: to show their contempt for
195 Injurious: hurtful, unjust
196 contrived: planned
197 bait: persecute
198 counsel: confidences
200 chid: scolded

203 artificial: skilled at making things
205 sampler: piece of embroidery
206 warbling of: singing
206 both in one key: in perfect harmony
208 incorporate: part of the same body
210 a union in partition: joined where they are picked
213–4 Two of the first ... with one crest: she uses terms from heraldry to talk about symbols used more than once to one person
215 rent: tear
215 asunder: apart

218 Our sex: all women

Hermia   I am amazed at your passionate words.   220
I scorn you not. It seems that you scorn me.

Helena   Have you not set Lysander, as in scorn,
To follow me and praise my eyes and face?
And made your other love, Demetrius,
Who even but now did spurn me with his foot,   225
To call me goddess, nymph, divine and rare,
Precious, celestial? Wherefore speaks he this
To her he hates? And wherefore doth Lysander
Deny your love (so rich within his soul)
And tender me, forsooth, affection,   230

225 even but now: just now
226 rare: exceptional
227 celestial: heavenly
227 Wherefore: why

230 tender: offer
230 forsooth: no, honestly

A

B

C

The lovers' quarrel, 2008.

A Demetrius, Helena, Lysander.
B Helena, Lysander and Demetrius (partly hidden), Hermia.
C Helena, Lysander, Demetrius, Hermia.

1 In Photo A what does Helena's expression suggest she feels about what is happening?
2 In Photo B how might Hermia have got in this position?
3 In Photo C what are Helena and Hermia doing with their right hands?
4 In each photo, explain who seems to be the aggressor.
5 These three photos were taken between lines 255–260 and 295–300. In which order were they taken? Quote from the text to support your answer.

Demetrius Oliver Boot; *Helena* Laura Rogers; *Hermia* Pippa Nixon; *Lysander* Christopher Brandon

Actor's view

Peter Bray
Lysander, 2012

With this potion, he can only think in absolutes – absolutes and extremes. He becomes the complete fundamentalist; in every direction he will chose the most extreme course of action. So, in love with Helena, he rips off all his clothes. On realising that Hermia's there and he doesn't like her it's not that he just goes off her and becomes indifferent; he despises her so much. He says, 'of all be hated, but the most of me.' She makes him physically sick; which is 100 percent in the opposite direction [to his previous feelings].

	But by your setting on, by your consent?
	What though I be not so in grace as you,
	So hung upon with love, so fortunate,
	But miserable most, to love unloved?
	This you should pity, rather than despise.
Hermia	I understand not what you mean by this.
Helena	Ay, do persever. Counterfeit sad looks,
	Make mouths upon me when I turn my back,
	Wink each at other, hold the sweet jest up.
	This sport, well carried, shall be chronicled.
	If you have any pity, grace, or manners,
	You would not make me such an argument.
	But fare ye well. 'Tis partly my own fault,
	Which death or absence soon shall remedy.
Lysander	Stay, gentle Helena, hear my excuse,
	My love, my life, my soul, fair Helena!
Helena	O excellent!
Hermia	Sweet, do not scorn her so.
Demetrius	If she cannot entreat, I can compel.
Lysander	Thou canst compel no more than she entreat.
	Thy threats have no more strength than her weak prayers.
	Helen, I love thee, by my life, I do.
	I swear by that which I will lose for thee,
	To prove him false, that says I love thee not.
Demetrius	I say I love thee more than he can do.
Lysander	If thou say so, withdraw and prove it too.
Demetrius	Quick, come!
Hermia	Lysander, whereto tends all this?
Lysander	*[Hermia clings to Lysander.]*
	Away, you Ethiope!
Demetrius	*[To Hermia.]* No, no. He'll
	Seem to break loose.
	[To Lysander.] Take on as you would follow,
	But yet come not? You are a tame man, go!
Lysander	Hang off thou cat, thou burr. Vile thing let loose,
	Or I will shake thee from me like a serpent.
Hermia	Why are you grown so rude? What change is this
	Sweet love?
Lysander	Thy love? Out, tawny Tartar, out!
	Out loathed medicine! O hated potion hence!
Hermia	Do you not jest?
Helena	Yes sooth, and so do you.
Lysander	Demetrius, I will keep my word with thee.

231 your setting on: you putting him up to it
232 grace: favour
234 miserable most: the most unhappy
235
237 Ay, do persever: that's it, go on
237 counterfeit: fake
238 Make mouths upon: pull faces at
240 **240 be chronicled:** be written about
242 an argument: a figure of fun
244 remedy: cure
245
248 If she cannot entreat, I can compel: If she can persuade you, I can force you
252 by that which I will lose for thee: by my life
255 **255 withdraw:** come away (to fight a duel)
256 whereto tends: what's the point of
257 Ethiope: Ethiopian (so dark-skinned; fair complexions were thought to be more beautiful)
258 Take on as: you're acting as if
259 tame man: coward
260 **260 Hang off:** let go
260 burr: rough seed-head that sticks to clothing
260 let loose: let go
262 rude: rough, unkind
263 Tartar: the Tartars of Central Asia were famous for their ferocity
264 loathed medicine: poison
264 potion: mixture
264 hence: go away
265 **265 Do you not jest?:** you're joking, aren't you?
265 sooth: truly

A

C

E

B

D

F

The lovers' quarrel, 2012.

In this scene Louise Collins' Hermia flipped from being clingy and confused to being in a furious rage. These photos (not in order) show some of the points in her journey. What is the correct order of the photos? They go with the following lines. Explain the reasons for your choices.

- line 181
- lines 261–3
- line 282
- line 298 and stage direction
- lines 322–4
- lines 340–2

Demetrius Richard James-Neale; *Helena* Carlyss Peer; *Hermia* Louise Collins; *Lysander* Peter Bray

Demetrius	I would I had your bond, for I perceive A weak bond holds you. I'll not trust your word.
Lysander	What, should I hurt her, strike her, kill her dead? Although I hate her, I'll not harm her so.
Hermia	What, can you do me greater harm than hate? Hate me? Wherefore? O me, what news, my love? Am not I Hermia? Are not you Lysander? I am as fair now as I was erewhile. Since night you loved me, yet since night you left me. Why, then you left me, O the gods forbid, In earnest, shall I say?
Lysander	Ay, by my life, And never did desire to see thee more. Therefore be out of hope, of question, of doubt. Be certain, nothing truer; 'tis no jest That I do hate thee and love Helena.
Hermia	O me! *[To Helena.]* You juggler, you canker-blossom, You thief of love! What, have you come by night And stolen my love's heart from him?
Helena	Fine, i'faith. Have you no modesty, no maiden shame, No touch of bashfulness? What, will you tear Impatient answers from my gentle tongue? Fie, fie, you counterfeit. You puppet, you!
Hermia	"Puppet"? Why so? Ay, that way goes the game. Now I perceive that she hath made compare Between our statures. She hath urged her height, And with her personage, her tall personage, Her height, forsooth, she hath prevailed with him. And are you grown so high in his esteem Because I am so dwarfish and so low? How low am I, thou painted maypole? Speak! How low am I? I am not yet so low But that my nails can reach unto thine eyes.

[She runs at Helena.]

Helena	I pray you, though you mock me, gentlemen, Let her not hurt me. I was never curst. I have no gift at all in shrewishness. I am a right maid for my cowardice. Let her not strike me. You perhaps may think, Because she is something lower than myself, That I can match her.
Hermia	Lower? Hark again.
Helena	Good Hermia, do not be so bitter with me. I evermore did love you Hermia, Did ever keep your counsels, never wronged you, Save that, in love unto Demetrius, I told him of your stealth unto this wood.

Glossary:
267 **I would:** I wish
267 **your bond:** your word
268 **A weak bond:** Hermia is holding onto him
269 **should I:** do you want me to
272 **O me:** an exclamation of misery
272 **what news:** what's going on
274 **erewhile:** before
275 **Since night:** when night fell
277 **In earnest:** in all seriousness
279 **be out of:** have no
282 **juggler:** trickster
282 **canker-blossom:** flower-eating grub
284 **Fine, i'faith:** oh, well done
288 **Fie, fie:** For shame
288 **counterfeit:** false friend
289 **Why so?:** so that's it?
291 **statures:** heights
292 **personage:** appearance
293 **prevailed with him:** won him over
294 **esteem:** opinion
295 **low:** short
296 **painted maypole:** tall, skinny person, covered in make-up
300 **curst:** bad-tempered
301 **in shrewishness:** for quarrelling
302 **right maid for:** a proper maiden because of
304 **something lower:** a bit shorter
305 **match her:** equal her in a fight
307 **evermore:** always
308 **Did ever keep your counsels:** kept all your secrets
309 **Save that:** except
309 **in love unto:** because I loved
310 **stealth unto:** running away into

FROM THE REHEARSAL ROOM...

WHO LOVES WHO?

- Read from line 320 to the exit of Lysander and Demetrius after line 339.
- Who loves who now?
1 Copy the diagram below, and draw arrows to show your answer. Use a different colour to show love as a result of the drug.

After Oberon drugs Demetrius (3.2)

Hermia	Helena

Lysander	Demetrius

Hermia and Helena, 2008.

In the 2008 production, Helena turned and ran off the stage (after line 343). Hermia chased her, then stopped, said line 344, and walked off.
If you were directing this scene, how would you stage lines 339 to 344? Explain your answer, referring to the text.

Pippa Nixon, Laura Rogers

FROM THE REHEARSAL ROOM...

DRUGWATCH

This is a role-play. Use the instructions on page 34. In groups, cast the Investigator, Oberon, Hermia, Helena, and the Observers.

- Oberon should study Act 3 Scene 2, lines 98–110; Hermia and Helena the *Working Cut* on page 60.
1 Who drugged who?
2 Who has been behaving strangely?

	He followed you, for love I followed him,	311	**for love:** because I was in love
	But he hath chid me hence, and threatened me	312	**chid me hence:** harshly told me to go away
	To strike me, spurn me, nay to kill me too.		
	And now, so you will let me quiet go,	314	**so:** if
	To Athens will I bear my folly back · 315		
	And follow you no further. Let me go.		
	You see how simple and how fond I am.	317	**fond:** foolish
Hermia	Why, get you gone! Who is't that hinders you?		
Helena	A foolish heart, that I leave here behind.		
Hermia	What, with Lysander?		
Helena	With Demetrius. · 320		
Lysander	Be not afraid, she shall not harm thee Helena.		
Demetrius	No, sir, she shall not, though you take her part.	322	**though:** even though
		322	**part:** side
Helena	O, when she is angry, she is keen and shrewd.	323	**keen:** bitter or sharp
	She was a vixen when she went to school,	323	**shrewd:** quarrelsome
	And though she be but little, she is fierce. · 325	324	**vixen:** female fox; fierce girl
Hermia	"Little" again? Nothing but "low" and "little"?		
	Why will you suffer her to flout me thus?	327	**suffer:** allow
	Let me come to her!	327	**flout:** insult
Lysander	Get you gone: you dwarf,		
	You minimus of hind'ring knot-grass made,	329	**minimus:** speck
	You bead, you acorn.	329	**hind'ring knot-grass:** creeping, clinging grass
Demetrius	You are too officious · 330	330–1	**officious In her behalf:** pushy about helping
	In her behalf that scorns your services.		
	Let her alone. Speak not of Helena,		
	Take not her part. For if thou dost intend		
	Never so little show of love to her,	334	**Never so little:** even the slightest
	Thou shalt a-buy it.		
Lysander	Now she holds me not. · 335	335	**a-buy it:** pay dearly for it
	Now follow, if thou dar'st, to try whose right,	336–7	**to try whose right … in Helena:** to duel to decide who will court Helena
	Of thine or mine, is most in Helena.		
Demetrius	Follow? Nay, I'll go with thee cheek by jowl.	338	**cheek by jowl:** side-by-side

Exit Lysander and Demetrius.

Hermia	You, mistress, all this coil is long of you.	339	**coil:** trouble
	Nay, go not back.	339	**long of you:** your fault
Helena	I will not trust you, I, · 340		
	Nor longer stay in your curst company.		
	Your hands than mine are quicker for a fray,	342	**a fray:** a fight
	My legs are longer though, to run away. *[She runs off.]*		
Hermia	I am amazed, and know not what to say. *She exits.*		

Oberon and Puck move forward.

Oberon	This is thy negligence. Still thou mistak'st, · 345		
	Or else committ'st thy knaveries wilfully.	346	**committ'st thy knaveries wilfully:** you're doing this deliberately
Puck	Believe me, king of shadows, I mistook.		
	Did not you tell me I should know the man		

Oberon and Puck: *A* 2008; *B* 2012.

1 Look at the body language in the photos. Who is in control? Give reasons for your answers.

2 Which of these two photos is most likely to have been taken between lines 347–349, and which between lines 366–369? Explain your answers with reference to the text.

A Tom Mannion, Michael Jibson; *B* Chook Sibtain, Fergal McElherron

By the Athenian garments he had on?
And so far blameless proves my enterprise,   350
That I have 'nointed an Athenian's eyes.
And so far am I glad it so did sort
As this their jangling I esteem a sport.

Oberon   Thou see'st these lovers seek a place to fight.
Hie therefore, Robin, overcast the night,   355
The starry welkin cover thou anon
With drooping fog as black as Acheron,
And lead these testy rivals so astray
As one come not within another's way.
Like to Lysander sometime frame thy tongue,   360
Then stir Demetrius up with bitter wrong.
And sometime rail thou like Demetrius,
And from each other look thou lead them thus,
Till o'er their brows death-counterfeiting sleep
With leaden legs and batty wings doth creep.   365
Then crush this herb into Lysander's eye,
Whose liquor hath this virtuous property,
To take from thence all error with his might,
And make his eyeballs roll with wonted sight.
When they next wake, all this derision   370
Shall seem a dream and fruitless vision.
And back to Athens shall the lovers wend,
With league whose date till death shall never end.
Whiles I in this affair do thee employ,
I'll to my Queen, and beg her Indian boy.   375
And then I will her charmèd eye release
From monster's view, and all things shall be peace.

Puck   My fairy lord, this must be done with haste,
For night's swift dragons cut the clouds full fast,
And yonder shines Aurora's harbinger,   380
At whose approach, ghosts, wandering here and there,
Troop home to churchyards. Damnèd spirits all,
That in crossways and floods have burial,
Already to their wormy beds are gone.
For fear lest day should look their shames upon,   385
They willfully themselves exile from light
And must for aye consort with black-browed night.

Oberon   But we are spirits of another sort.
I with the morning's love have oft made sport,
And like a forester, the groves may tread   390
Even till the eastern gate all fiery-red,
Opening on Neptune with fair blessèd beams,
Turns into yellow gold his salt green streams.
But, notwithstanding, haste, make no delay,
We may effect this business yet ere day.   *[He exits.]* 395

Puck   Up and down, up and down,
I will lead them up and down.
I am fear'd in field and town.
Goblin, lead them up and down.
Here comes one.   400

---

350 **my enterprise:** my actions

352 **so did sort:** turned out this way
353 **jangling:** squabbling
353 **I esteem a sport:** I think is a good laugh
355 **Hie:** hurry
356 **welkin:** sky
357 **drooping:** falling
357 **Acheron:** a river in the Underworld (Hell in Greek myths)
358 **testy:** bad-tempered
359 **As one come not within another's way:** so they never meet
360 **frame thy tongue:** sound
362 **rail:** rant
363 **look thou:** be sure to
365 **batty:** bat-like
367 **virtuous property:** beneficial effect
368 **his:** its
369 **his eyeballs roll with wonted sight:** him look, and feel, as he used to
370 **derision:** scornful squabbling
372 **wend:** make their way
373 **With league ... shall never end:** with lifelong relationships formed

376 **charmèd:** bewitched

379 **dragons:** said to pull the moon's chariot
380 **Aurora's harbinger:** the morning star, first sign of dawn
383 **crossways:** crossroads, where suicides were buried
383 **floods:** rivers or seas where the drowned who were not found are buried

387 **for aye:** for ever

389 **I with the morning's ... made sport:** I'm quite happy to be up at dawn
391 **the eastern gate:** the sky in the east, where the sun rises
392 **Opening on Neptune:** shines on the sea (Neptune was the Roman god of the sea)
394 **notwithstanding:** despite all that

399 **Goblin:** he's referring to himself

Enter Lysander.

Lysander Where art thou, proud Demetrius? Speak thou now.

Puck *[Imitating Demetrius' voice.]*
Here villain, drawn and ready. Where art thou?

Lysander I will be with thee straight.

Puck Follow me, then,
To plainer ground. *[Exit Lysander, following the voice.]*

Enter Demetrius.

Demetrius Lysander, speak again!
Thou runaway, thou coward, art thou fled? 405
Speak! In some bush? Where dost thou hide thy head?

Puck *[Imitating Lysander's voice.]*
Thou coward, art thou bragging to the stars?
Telling the bushes that thou look'st for wars,
And wilt not come? Come recreant, come, thou child,
I'll whip thee with a rod. He is defiled 410
That draws a sword on thee.

Demetrius Yea, art thou there?

Puck Follow my voice, we'll try no manhood here. *They exit.*

[Enter Lysander.]

Lysander He goes before me, and still dares me on.
When I come where he calls, then he is gone.
The villain is much lighter-heeled than I, 415
I followed fast, but faster he did fly,
That fallen am I in dark uneven way,
And here will rest me.
He lies down. Come, thou gentle day,
For if but once thou show me thy grey light,
I'll find Demetrius and revenge this spite. *[He sleeps.]* 420

Enter Puck and Demetrius.

Puck *[Imitating Lysander's voice.]*
Ho, ho, ho! Coward, why com'st thou not?

Demetrius Abide me, if thou dar'st. For well I wot
Thou runn'st before me, shifting every place,
And dar'st not stand, nor look me in the face.
Where art thou now?

Puck Come hither, I am here. 425

Demetrius Nay, then, thou mock'st me. Thou shalt buy this dear,
If ever I thy face by daylight see.
Now, go thy way. Faintness constraineth me
To measure out my length on this cold bed. *[Lies down.]*
By day's approach look to be visited. *[He sleeps.]* 430

Enter Helena.

Helena O weary night, O long and tedious night,
Abate thy hours! Shine comforts from the east,

---

402 **drawn:** with my sword drawn

403 **straight:** straight away
404 **plainer:** flatter, more open

408 **look'st for wars:** want to fight
409 **recreant:** coward
410 **with a rod:** beat you like a schoolboy
410 **defiled:** shamed

412 **we'll try no manhood here:** this isn't the right place to fight

415 **lighter-heeled:** quicker on his feet

417 **That:** and now

420 **revenge this spite:** punish him for leading me here

422 **Abide me:** wait for me
422 **well I wot:** I know quite well
423 **before:** in front of

426 **buy this dear:** pay for this

428 **go thy way:** do what you like
428 **constraineth:** forces
429 **measure out my length:** lie down
430 **look to be visited:** expect to be found
432 **Abate:** shorten
432 **Shine comforts from the east:** send comforting daylight

B

A (page 72): **Puck gets ready to squeeze the juice in Lysander's eyes, 2008.
B:** Puck uses his magic to raise Lysander's sleeping head up, so he can squeeze the juice in his eyes, 2012.

1 In Photo A, what has Puck got in each hand?

2 Both productions start with the same stage direction. Both have added their own interpretation. What effect do you think the interpretation will have on the audience in each case? Explain your answer.

A Michael Jibson, Christopher Brandon
B Fergal McElherron, Peter Bray

FROM THE REHEARSAL ROOM...

STATUS LINE UP

Work in groups. Like the exercise on page 62, this is also about status.

- In the world of the wood, discuss how much status Oberon, Puck, and the lovers have. In a status line, with the most important on the left, where would you put each of them?

- Now add Titania to the line – where should she go?

- Now add the Fairies to the line – where should they go?

- Add Bottom to the line – where should he go?

- Compare your lines with others – do you agree?

1 List the characters in this exercise in order of importance, highest status first.
   (Bottom, lovers, Oberon, Puck, Titania.)

2 Explain why you think your top ranking character is the most important.

3 Explain why you think your lowest ranking character is the least important.

4 Which characters are easiest to put in order? Why do you think this is?

5 Which characters are hardest to put in order? Why do you think this is?

Director's Note, 3.2

✔ Puck tells Oberon about Titania and Bottom.

✔ Oberon sees Puck has drugged the wrong man. He drugs Demetrius; Puck fetches Helena.

✔ Lysander and Helena wake Demetrius. The men quarrel about who loves Helena most, while she accuses them of making fun of her.

✔ Hermia arrives, thrilled to find Lysander. When he swears he now loves Helena, Hermia blames Helena and attacks her. The men go off to fight, Helena runs away, followed by Hermia.

✔ Oberon sends Puck to fetch the lovers, make them sleep, and give Lysander an antidote.

That I may back to Athens by daylight,
From these that my poor company detest.
And sleep, that sometimes shuts up sorrow's eye,   435
Steal me awhile from mine own company.

She lies down and sleeps.

Puck   Yet but three? Come one more,
Two of both kinds make up four.
Here she comes, curst and sad.   **439 curst:** cross
Cupid is a knavish lad,   440
Thus to make poor females mad.

Enter Hermia.

Hermia   Never so weary, never so in woe,
Bedabbled with the dew and torn with briers,   **443 Bedabbled:** splattered
I can no further crawl, no further go.   **443 briers:** brambles
My legs can keep no pace with my desires.   445   **445 can keep no pace with my**
Here will I rest me, till the break of day.   *[Lies down.]*   **desires:** can't keep going
Heavens shield Lysander, if they mean a fray.   **447 a fray:** to fight

[She sleeps.]

Puck   On the ground
Sleep sound.
I'll apply   450
To your eye,
Gentle lover, remedy.
[Squeezing the juice over Lysander's eyes.]
When thou wak'st,
Thou tak'st
True delight   455
In the sight
Of thy former lady's eye.
And the country proverb known,
That every man should take his own,
In your waking shall be shown.   460   **460 shall be shown:** will be proved
Jack shall have Jill,   right
Nought shall go ill,   **462 Nought shall go ill:** nothing will
The man shall have his mare again, and all shall be well.   go wrong
                                                                                                   463 The man shall have his mare
Exit Puck, leaving the lovers sleeping on the stage.   **again:** proverb for things turning
                                                                                                   out all right

---

Actor's view

Fergal McElherron
Puck, 2012

As Puck I used to click my fingers at every instruction, so the person I was putting the spell on became totally under my control for those moments. So it would be click, and he'd sit upright and then another click would open his eyes. I would get the flower and press the petals to get some of the juice out of it, then sprinkle it on Lysander's eyes – not smearing it into the pupils but as if I was sprinkling pepper or salt. Peter would then react quite strongly to it – the eyes would pop wide open. The casting of the spell was quite physically intense.

SHAKESPEARE'S WORLD

Clowns, Will Kemp, and Bottom

Shakespeare's company included a clown. We know he played Bottom, because some of the original stage directions say *Clown* when they mean *Bottom*. When Shakespeare wrote *A Midsummer Night's Dream*, the clown was Will Kemp, one of the most famous actors in England. Clowns often added to what was in the text, and the crowd enjoyed the wit of these celebrated comedians. So, as Bottom, Kemp probably added several lines, and they would have been different every time.

Every play, whether it was a comedy, tragedy, or history, ended with a *jig*. This was a dance and a comic song. Kemp was the star of the jig, and his jigs were as popular as Shakespeare's plays. Perhaps this is why Theseus asks Bottom to dance in the final scene. Other roles played by Kemp were Dogberry in *Much Ado About Nothing*, Peter in *Romeo and Juliet*, and Falstaff in *Henry IV*. Kemp left the company in 1599. Shakespeare's clown parts were different in his plays written after 1599, as he was writing for someone else.

'Come, sit thee down upon this flowery bed,
While I thy amiable cheeks do coy'

Titania and her Fairies make Bottom feel special, 2008.

1 How did this production deal with:
   a) the last stage direction of the previous scene?
   b) the stage direction in the text in the first two lines of this scene, quoted above?

2 What impression have the director and designer tried to create by the way they have staged this scene?

3 How would you stage the opening of this scene?

Siobhan Redmond, Bethan Walker, Paul Hunter, Adam Burton, Sian Williams, and, sleeping, Christopher Brandon, Pippa Nixon, Laura Rogers, Oliver Boot

ACT 4 SCENE 1

Lysander, Demetrius, Helena, and Hermia are still sleeping.

*Enter Titania, Bottom, Peaseblossom, Cobweb, Moth
Mustardseed, and other Fairies, and Oberon, unseen,
behind them.*

Titania	Come, sit thee down upon this flowery bed,
	While I thy amiable cheeks do coy,
	And stick musk-roses in thy sleek smooth head,
	And kiss thy fair large ears, my gentle joy.

2 **amiable:** loveable
2 **coy:** stroke

| Bottom | Where's Peaseblossom? | 5 |

| Peaseblossom | Ready. |

| Bottom | Scratch my head, Peaseblossom. Where's Mounsieur Cobweb? |

7 **Mounsieur:** Bottom mispronounces the French for 'Mr'

| Cobweb | Ready. |

Bottom	Mounsieur Cobweb, good mounsieur, get you your	10
	weapons in your hand, and kill me a red-hipped
	humble-bee on the top of a thistle, and, good mounsieur,
	bring me the honey-bag. Do not fret yourself too much
	in the action, mounsieur. And good mounsieur have a care
	the honey-bag break not. I would be loath to have you	15
	overflown with a honey-bag signior. *[Exit Cobweb.]*
	Where's Mounsieur Mustardseed?

13 **fret:** trouble
14 **in the action:** doing it
15 **I would be loath:** I wouldn't like
16 **overflown with:** drenched by
16 **signior:** Italian for 'Mr'

| Mustardseed | Ready. |

| Bottom | Give me your neaf, Mounsieur Mustardseed. Pray you, |
| | leave your courtesy, good mounsieur. | 20 |

19 **neaf:** hand
20 **leave your courtesy:** stop bowing

| Mustardseed | What's your will? |

Bottom	Nothing, good mounsieur, but to help Cavalery Cobweb
	to scratch. I must to the barber's mounsieur, for
	methinks I am marvellous hairy about the face. And I
	am such a tender ass, if my hair do but tickle me, I	25
	must scratch.

22 **Cavalery:** he means 'Cavaliere' – an Italian word for an officer
24 **marvellous:** amazingly

| Titania | What, wilt thou hear some music, my sweet love? |

| Bottom | I have a reasonable good ear in music. Let's have the |
| | tongs and the bones. |

29 **tongs:** metal musical instrument, like a modern triangle
29 **bones:** pieces of bone played like modern castanets

Simple rural music starts.

| Titania | Or say, sweet love, what thou desir'st to eat. | 30 |

Bottom	Truly, a peck of provender. I could munch your good
	dry oats. Methinks I have a great desire to a bottle of
	hay. Good hay, sweet hay, hath no fellow.

31 **a peck of provender:** a portion of animal food
32 **bottle:** bundle
33 **hath no fellow:** there's nothing like it

| Titania | I have a venturous fairy, that shall seek |
| | The squirrel's hoard, and fetch thee new nuts. | 35 |

34 **venturous:** daring

Bottom	I had rather have a handful or two of dried peas. But, I
	pray you, let none of your people stir me, I have an
	exposition of sleep come upon me.

37 **stir:** disturb
38 **exposition of:** he means 'disposition to' – desire to

Bottom, Titania, and Oberon, 2012.

1 Which line or lines were being spoken when this photo was taken?
Quote from the text to support your answer.

2 Compare this with the photos on page 58, 70, and 74. What is
different about the way this production shows the use of the flower?

Russell Layton, Emma Pallant, Chook Sibtain

Titania Sleep thou, and I will wind thee in my arms.
Fairies, begone, and be all ways away.   *[Exit Faries.]* 40
So doth the woodbine, the sweet honeysuckle,
Gently entwist. The female ivy so
Enrings the barky fingers of the elm.
O, how I love thee! How I dote on thee!
[They sleep, on a different part of the stage to the lovers.]

Enter Puck, going to Oberon.

Oberon Welcome, good Robin. See'st thou this sweet sight? 45
Her dotage now I do begin to pity.
For meeting her of late behind the wood,
Seeking sweet favours for this hateful fool,
I did upbraid her and fall out with her.
For she his hairy temples then had rounded 50
With coronet of fresh and fragrant flowers.
And that same dew, which sometime on the buds
Was wont to swell like round and orient pearls,
Stood now within the pretty flowerets' eyes,
Like tears that did their own disgrace bewail. 55
When I had at my pleasure taunted her,
And she in mild terms begged my patience,
I then did ask of her her changeling child,
Which straight she gave me, and her fairy sent
To bear him to my bower in Fairy Land. 60
And now I have the boy, I will undo
This hateful imperfection of her eyes.
And, gentle Puck, take this transformèd scalp,
From off the head of this Athenian swain,
That he, awaking when the other do, 65
May all to Athens back again repair,
And think no more of this night's accidents
But as the fierce vexation of a dream.
But first I will release the Fairy Queen.
[He squeezes the flower on Titania's eyes.]
Be as thou wast wont to be, 70
See as thou wast wont to see.
Dian's bud, or Cupid's flower
Hath such force and blessèd power.
Now my Titania, wake you, my sweet queen.

Titania My Oberon, what visions have I seen! 75
Methought I was enamoured of an ass.

Oberon There lies your love.

Titania   How came these things to pass?
O, how mine eyes do loathe his visage now!

Oberon Silence awhile. Robin, take off this head.
Titania, music call, and strike more dead 80
Than common sleep of all these five the sense.

Titania Music, ho! Music such as charmeth sleep.

The rural music stops.

Puck *[Taking off the ass-head.]*
Now, when thou wak'st, with thine own fool's eyes peep.

---

40 **and be all ways away:** scatter in all directions
41 **woodbine:** bindweed, which twines around honeysuckle
43 **Enrings:** wraps around
43 **barky fingers:** branches and twigs
46 **dotage:** wild infatuation
48 **favours:** presents
49 **upbraid:** scold
50 **temples:** forehead
51 **coronet:** a crown
53 **Was wont to:** used to
53 **orient:** from the east
54 **flowerets:** little flowers
55 **bewail:** weep at
59 **straight:** at once
63 **transformèd scalp:** the ass's head
64 **swain:** man
65 **other:** others
66 **repair:** return
68 **fierce vexation:** upsetting memory
70 **thou wast wont:** you used
72 **Dian's bud:** the antidote
72 **Cupid's flower:** the original juice
76 **enamoured of:** in love with
77 **pass:** happen
78 **visage:** face
80–1 **strike more dead ... the sense:** make Bottom and the lovers sleep very deeply

FROM THE REHEARSAL ROOM...

DRUGWATCH

- This is a role-play. Use the instructions on page 34. Cast the Investigator, Oberon, and the Observers.
- Oberon should study lines 46–62, and 69–91.
- **1** Who drugged who?
- **2** Have Oberon's motives changed?

A

B

Puck and the Fairies dance, after Oberon and Titania have left the stage, 2008.

In *A Midsummer Night's Dream*, the world of the Fairies can be seen to shadow the world of the humans. Most productions of the play underline this by the use of doubling – having actors play more than one role. So, often the same actor plays Theseus and Oberon, while another plays both Hippolyta and Titania. All three productions featured in this edition doubled Theseus with Oberon and Hippolyta with Titania, so they could not be on stage at the same time.

Look at what happens on stage between lines 100 and 105. Why might the director have added a dance at this point? Explain your answer.

Top, l–r Sian Williams, Adam Burton, Peter Bankolé, Michael Jibson, Bethan Walker

Oberon   Sound, music!   *[Different music starts.]*
                    Come, my queen, take hands with me,
          And rock the ground whereon these sleepers be.   85
                    [Oberon and Titania dance.]
          Now, thou and I are new in amity,
          And will tomorrow midnight, solemnly
          Dance in Duke Theseus' house triumphantly,
          And bless it to all fair prosperity.
          There shall the pairs of faithful lovers be   90
          Wedded, with Theseus, all in jollity.

Puck   Fairy king, attend and mark,
          I do hear the morning lark.

Oberon   Then my queen, in silence sad,
          Trip we after the night's shade.   95
          We the globe can compass soon,
          Swifter than the wandering moon.

Titania   Come my lord, and in our flight,
          Tell me how it came this night
          That I sleeping here was found   100
          With these mortals on the ground.
                    Exit Oberon, Titania, and Puck.
                    The lovers and Bottom continue to sleep.
                    Hunting horns sound offstage.
                    Enter Theseus, Hippolyta, Egeus, and followers.

Theseus   Go one of you, find out the forester,
          For now our observation is performed,
          And since we have the vaward of the day,
          My love shall hear the music of my hounds.   105
          Uncouple in the western valley, let them go.
          Dispatch I say, and find the forester.   *[Exit a servant.]*
          We will, fair queen, up to the mountain's top,
          And mark the musical confusion
          Of hounds and echo in conjunction.   110

Hippolyta I was with Hercules and Cadmus once,
          When in a wood of Crete they bayed the bear
          With hounds of Sparta. Never did I hear
          Such gallant chiding, for, besides the groves,
          The skies, the fountains, every region near   115
          Seemed all one mutual cry. I never heard
          So musical a discord, such sweet thunder.

Theseus   My hounds are bred out of the Spartan kind,
          So flewed, so sanded, and their heads are hung
          With ears that sweep away the morning dew,   120
          Crook-kneed and dew-lapped, like Thessalian bulls,
          Slow in pursuit, but matched in mouth like bells,
          Each under each. A cry more tuneable
          Was never holla'd to, nor cheered with horn,
          In Crete, in Sparta, nor in Thessaly.   125
          Judge when you hear.   *[He sees the lovers.]*
                    But, soft, what nymphs are these?

---

86 **new in amity:** friends again

89 **to all fair prosperity:** so they do well

92 **attend:** listen
92 **mark:** take note

94 **sad:** serious
95 **Trip we after:** Let's quickly follow
96 **compass:** go around

103 **observation is performed:** May Day ceremonies are finished
104 **we have the vaward of the day:** we were up so early
106 **Uncouple:** let them loose
107 **Dispatch:** hurry
108 **We will:** we'll go
110 **in conjunction:** at the same time
111 **Hercules:** mythical Greek hero
111 **Cadmus:** mythical Greek king of Thebes
112 **bayed:** cornered ·
113 **hounds of Sparta:** a famous breed of hunting dog
114 **gallant chiding:** brave barking
116 **one mutual cry:** a single sound
118 **kind:** breed
119 **So flewed:** with the same folds on their cheeks
119 **So sanded:** the same sandy colour
121 **dew-lapped:** with loose folds of neck skin
121 **Thessalian:** from Thessaly, in Greece
122-3 **matched in mouth ... Each under each:** with harmonious barks
123 **tuneable:** musical
124 **holla'd:** hunted to
126 **soft:** wait a minute
126 **nymphs:** woodland spirits

SHAKESPEARE'S WORLD

Betrothal

Usually, before people got married in Shakespeare's time, they were betrothed to one another first. This happened after any courtship and marital negotiations between the groom and the bride's father were finished (see page 8). It was far more serious than an engagement is today. A betrothal was a way to show the community that a couple would marry. While not every couple had a betrothal ceremony, it was an important occasion. People were encouraged to have one. The man and woman would swear before God and their family and friends that they would marry. Many people had a formal ceremony in a church with a priest, much like a wedding. The couple would take hands and exchange vows with one another to show they were serious in their commitment to marry. This was a contract that neither was supposed to break. Some couples even used a lawyer to draw up an actual contract. Now the community knew that the couple were serious and that they would marry. Some couples even treated each other as husband and wife after a betrothal. Demetrius says he is betrothed to Helena. This was legally binding. Most people in Shakespeare's original audience would strongly disapprove of breaking a betrothal.

A

B

FROM THE REHEARSAL ROOM...

DRUGWATCH

This is a role-play. Use the instructions on page 34. In groups, cast the Investigator, Demetrius, and the Observers.

- Demetrius should study lines 169–185.
1 What has changed?
2 Why? (Look back at the results of your Drugwatch role-play on page 75.)

Theseus, the lovers, and Egeus (behind Theseus in *B*), 2012.

1 What is Theseus doing in Photo B?
2 Which photo was taken earlier in the scene?
3 Which of Theseus' lines has the director cut to allow him to stage the scene as he has in Photo B? Quote from the text to support your answer.

Top, l–r Richard James-Neale, Carlyss Peer, Chook Sibtain, Louise Collins, Peter Bray, William Oxborrow

Egeus	My lord, this is my daughter here asleep,
	And this Lysander, this Demetrius is,
	This Helena, old Nedar's Helena.
	I wonder of their being here together.

130

Theseus	No doubt they rose up early to observe
	The rite of May, and hearing our intent,
	Came here in grace of our solemnity.
	But speak Egeus, is not this the day
	That Hermia should give answer of her choice?

135

133 **in grace of our solemnity:** to attend our celebrations

Egeus	It is, my lord.
Theseus	Go, bid the huntsmen wake them with their horns.
	Exit servant. Horns offstage, Lysander, Demetrius, Helena,
	and Hermia wake up; then a shout offstage makes them start.
	Good morrow friends. Saint Valentine is past,
	Begin these wood-birds but to couple now?

138 **Saint Valentine:** Saint Valentine's Day, 14 February, traditionally thought to be when birds choose mates

139 **couple:** pair off

Lysander	Pardon, my lord. *[The lovers kneel to Theseus.]*
Theseus	I pray you all, stand up.

140

	I know you two are rival enemies.
	How comes this gentle concord in the world,
	That hatred is so far from jealousy,
	To sleep by hate, and fear no enmity?

142 **gentle concord:** friendliness
143 **jealousy:** suspicion
144 **by hate ... no enmity:** beside the person who hates him with no fear of harm

Lysander	My lord, I shall reply amazedly,
	Half sleep, half waking. But as yet, I swear,
	I cannot truly say how I came here.
	But as I think, (for truly would I speak)
	And now do I bethink me, so it is,
	I came with Hermia hither. Our intent
	Was to be gone from Athens, where we might
	Without the peril of the Athenian law —

145

150

148 **truly would I speak:** I want to tell the exact truth
149 **now do I bethink me, so it is:** I now remember
150 **hither:** here

Egeus	Enough, enough, my lord. You have enough.
	I beg the law, the law, upon his head.
	They would have stolen away. — They would, Demetrius,
	Thereby to have defeated you and me.
	You of your wife, and me of my consent,
	Of my consent, that she should be your wife.

155

156 **Thereby:** by doing so
156 **defeated:** cheated

Demetrius	My lord, fair Helen told me of their stealth,
	Of this their purpose hither to this wood,
	And I in fury hither followed them,
	Fair Helena in fancy following me.
	But my good lord, I wot not by what power,
	But by some power it is, my love to Hermia,
	Melted as the snow, seems to me now
	As the remembrance of an idle gaud
	Which in my childhood I did dote upon.
	And all the faith, the virtue of my heart,
	The object and the pleasure of mine eye,
	Is only Helena. To her, my lord,
	Was I betrothed ere I saw Hermia.
	But like in sickness did I loathe this food,
	But as in health, come to my natural taste,

160

165

170

159 **stealth:** secretly running away

162 **in fancy:** because of love
163 **I wot not:** I don't know

166 **remembrance:** memory
166 **idle gaud:** cheap toy

172 **like in sickness:** just as if I was sick
173 **But as in health ... taste:** but when well, my normal appetite is restored

Bottom, during his speech at the end of this scene, 2008.

1 Pick a short quotation from this speech that could be used as a caption for this photo.

2 Explain how the actor's expression and body language fit with the quotation you have chosen.

Paul Hunter

WHO LOVES WHO?

Read from line 169–185 and 196–209.

• Who loves who now?

1 Copy the diagram below, drawing arrows to show your answer. Use a different colour to show love caused by the drug.

After Puck un-drugs Lysander (4.1)

Hermia	Helena
Lysander	Demetrius

Director's Note, 4.1

✔ (The lovers sleep on stage.)

✔ Titania is besotted with Bottom. They fall asleep.

✔ Oberon gives Titania the antidote, and wakes her. They are reconciled.

✔ Puck restores Bottom's head.

✔ The Fairies leave.

✔ Theseus and Hippolyta are hunting. Theseus sees the lovers and wakes them.

✔ Outraged that Hermia is with Lysander, Egeus demands Theseus punish them. Demetrius says he no longer wants to marry Hermia, but now loves Helena again.

✔ Theseus overrules Egeus, and orders the two pairs of lovers should marry when he and Hippolyta do.

✔ Bottom wakes, thinks the ass's head was a dream, and goes to find the other Mechanicals.

✔ Is everybody now back to their normal state?

Actor's view

Louise Collins
Hermia, 2012

For Hermia and Helena, that scene is interesting, because we don't have anything to say. The boys get us out of the situation, but I think actually we are left dumbfounded. I find that scene quite emotional, because I'd look at Lysander and I'd think, 'Well, do you love me now?' And then I'd look at Helena going, 'I'm really sorry about that'. And then my rage at Demetrius melts. Bill [the director] in rehearsals would say you can't remember the night, it's like you have got this really bad headache and everything's a bit blurry and you can't quite think what happened. Did it happen? The line is, 'I see these things with parted eye, when everything seems doubled.' You know, when you wake up from a nightmare, and you're not sure if it happened; I think it's that state. You have memories, images in the head, mixed emotions, but absolutely relieved that it's all going to be okay as well.

Now I do wish it, love it, long for it,
And will for evermore be true to it.   175

Theseus Fair lovers, you are fortunately met.
Of this discourse we more will hear anon.
Egeus, I will overbear your will,
For in the temple, by and by with us
These couples shall eternally be knit.   180
And, for the morning now is something worn,
Our purposed hunting shall be set aside.
Away with us to Athens, three and three,
We'll hold a feast in great solemnity.
Come Hippolyta.   185

Exit Theseus, Hippolyta, Egeus and followers.

Demetrius These things seem small and undistinguishable,
Like far off mountains turned into clouds.

Hermia Methinks I see these things with parted eye,
When every thing seems double.

Helena   So methinks.   190
And I have found Demetrius like a jewel,
Mine own, and not mine own.

Demetrius   Are you sure
That we are awake? It seems to me
That yet we sleep, we dream. Do not you think
The Duke was here, and bid us follow him?   195

Hermia Yea, and my father.

Helena   And Hippolyta.

Lysander And he did bid us follow to the temple.

Demetrius Why then we are awake. Let's follow him,
And by the way let us recount our dreams.

Exit lovers. Bottom wakes up.

Bottom When my cue comes, call me, and I will answer. My   200
next is, "Most fair Pyramus." Heigh-ho! Peter Quince?
Flute, the bellows-mender? Snout, the tinker?
Starveling? God's my life! Stolen hence, and left me
asleep. I have had a most rare vision. I have had a
dream, past the wit of man to say what dream it was.   205
Man is but an ass, if he go about to expound this dream.
Methought I was—there is no man can tell what.
Methought I was,—and methought I had ... (but man is
but a patched fool, if he will offer to say what
methought I had). The eye of man hath not heard, the   210
ear of man hath not seen, man's hand is not able to
taste, his tongue to conceive, nor his heart to report,
what my dream was. I will get Peter Quince to write a
ballad of this dream. It shall be called *Bottom's Dream*,
because it hath no bottom. And I will sing it in the   215
latter end of a play, before the Duke. Peradventure, to
make it the more gracious, I shall sing it at her death.

Exit Bottom.

177 **discourse:** story
177 **anon:** later
178 **overbear your will:** overrule you
179 **by and by:** soon
180 **eternally be knit:** be married
181 **for:** seeing as
181 **something worn:** almost over

188 **Methinks:** it seems to me
188 **with parted eye:** out of focus

194 **yet we sleep:** we're still sleeping

199 **by the way:** on the way
199 **recount:** tell each other

203 **God's my life!:** God save my life – a mild oath
203 **hence:** God away from here
204 **rare vision:** amazing, vivid dream
205 **past the wit ... what dream it was:** beyond understanding
206 **go about to expound:** tried to explain
209 **a patched fool:** a king's jester (they wore patchwork clothes)
209 **offer:** try
212 **conceive:** imagine
214 **ballad:** song
215 **it hath no bottom:** you can't get to the bottom of it
215-6 **in the latter end:** towards the end of
216 **Peradventure:** perhaps
217 **gracious:** pleasing
217 **her:** Thisbe's

EXAMINER'S NOTES, 4.1

These questions help you to explore many aspects of *A Midsummer Night's Dream*. Support each answer by reference to the text. At GCSE, your teacher will tell you which aspects are relevant to how your Shakespeare response will be assessed.

USING THE VIDEO

Exploring interpretation and performance

If you have looked at the video extracts in Dynamic Learning, try this question.

Discovering the four young lovers in the wood, Egeus is still angry, and asks Theseus to use the law to punish Lysander for taking his daughter away. When Theseus has heard Demetrius tell of his love for Helena, not Hermia, he tells Egeus 'I will overbear your will' and announces that the couples shall 'eternally be knit' in marriage.

How, without any words, does the actor playing Hermia and the actor playing Egeus convey feelings or motives at this point?

Do you think the audience response at this silent moment expresses sympathy or sadness for Hermia or for Egeus?

EXAMINER'S TIP

Writing about drama

Show that you understand why Shakespeare uses dramatic devices; e.g. 'Shakespeare makes Bottom say he would like "a bottle of hay" (lines 32–33). This is ironic because he doesn't realise that he has been turned into an ass, and is expressing his fondness for what an ass would consider a treat.'

❶ Character and plot development

This scene resolves all three plots as it reunites Oberon and Titania, the young lovers, and Bottom and the Mechanicals. If Shakespeare's only wish was to conclude a romantic drama this could be a final act showing that although love does not always 'run smooth', things turn out well in the end. As it is, he ties up aspects of the plot here and keeps the best laughs for this comedy with the single scene of Act 5.

1. How does Shakespeare bring together different parts of the plots in the play in this scene?
2. In what ways has Shakespeare brought about a change in Titania so she is no longer proud and independent, but besotted with Bottom in the first 44 lines of this scene?
3. What does Oberon's speech at lines 45–74 show about his change of feelings and attitude to Titania when she has been released from his magic spell?
4. How does Titania's response to Oberon contrast with her attitude in Act 2 Scene 1?
5. Shakespeare makes Egeus still angry before he hears Demetrius (still drugged) explain that his love has returned to Helena. Egeus says nothing then or when Theseus rules that the reunited pairs of lovers should be wed. What do you think Shakespeare wants the audience to make of this (lines 153–185)?
6. Shakespeare ends the scene with Bottom waking up. How does his speech here link with the previous events in the wood and with what is to follow in Act 5?

❷ Characterisation and voice: dramatic language

One of Shakespeare's skills as a dramatist is his exploitation of speech characteristics. These can convey the genuine feelings and attitudes of a character, or make them very different from what we know of the character. Both are evident in this scene.

7. In his normal life, Bottom is an ordinary working man. How does Shakespeare show him enjoying his unusual status with servants and Titania in lines 1–44?
8. How many examples can you find of Shakespeare getting in a joke based on Bottom's unawareness that he has an ass's head on his shoulders in lines 1–44?
9. What makes Titania seem a sensuous and exotic part of the natural world around her in lines 1–44?

EXAMINER'S NOTES, 4.1

3 Themes and ideas

This scene leaves the audience feeling that all is well that ends well. Love is presented as something that can survive setbacks and complications – which is why this play turns the situation into comedy rather than tragedy.

10 In what ways have the characters in this scene experienced that 'the course of true love never did run smooth'?

11 In what ways can some of the characters be described as changed and coming to their senses as they leave the wood?

4 Performance

Dramatic irony can please the audience because it makes them think they know more than the characters on stage. At the opening of this scene there is lots of scope for having the invisible Oberon react to what he sees.

12 What would you do to make *'Oberon, unseen, behind them'* (opening stage directions) an active part of the scene even though he has no lines?

13 What music might you choose for the stage directions *'Simple country music starts'* (line 30) and *'Different music starts'* (line 83) and how might each choice add to the scene?

14 What would you do to make the Fairies part of the comedy in this scene?

15 How might you use sound or light effects to make the use of magic flower juice theatrically interesting in lines 69–74?

5 Contexts and responses

On stage, the play has to convey a believable sense of different settings, some of the real world and some of the world of the supernatural. This can be done with sets and props, or with music, but language is Shakespeare's main resource.

16 What makes Theseus's first speech in this scene remind us of the world he belongs to, and his status in it (lines 102–126)?

17 What makes Bottom's speech in lines 200–217 remind us of the world he belongs to, and his status in it?

6 Reflecting on the scene

18 *'Something for everyone.'* Show how *A Midsummer Night's Dream* provides a variety of theatrical entertainment to please the widest audience.

19 In Act 3 Scene 2 line 115 Shakespeare gives Puck the words: 'what fools these mortals be!' As the play has developed, do you think Shakespeare has made all of the mortals appear foolish?

20 In what ways has your response to this scene been influenced by performance on stage, on screen or in the classroom?

EXAMINER'S TIP

A good response

A good response may refer to effects on the character on stage and then to effects on people in the audience.

For example, the effect of this scene on Bottom is that he imagines he has found himself in some kind of paradise.

The effect on the audience is that they know Oberon is using Bottom to play a trick on Titania, and once the trick has worked, he will be turned back into his usual self. The audience will find it amusing that Bottom, who thinks he can act any part, has been cast by a spell into another role without knowing it.

EXAMINER'S TIP

Writing about drama

Sometimes the success of a performance comes from what the audience sees, not just what it hears. Writing about visual business such as choosing a visual or sound effect to accompany each use of the magic flower-juice shows that you are thinking about how a text may be developed for performance.

EXAMINER'S TIP

Reflecting on the scene

Writing about dramatic techniques can be improved by linking to performance. Show how your understanding has developed by seeing the text performed on stage or screen, or through performance of an aspect of the scene yourself or as part of a group.

Actor's view

Peter Bray
Flute/Thisbe, 2012

The guy might be dead – or at the very worst, he's simply gone. There's no tracking him down, so it's hugely depressing; they're not going to be able to do this play at all if the man playing Pyramus doesn't turn up. And then, in that moment of rock bottom, there's a cry off stage, which becomes louder and closer, which sounds like Bottom, but surely it can't be. The way I played it, Flute turns round; to see this wonderful, wonderful, wonderful man has returned. Seemingly fit and happy and full of beans. And he [Bottom] says, 'Where are these lads? Where are these hearts?' which becomes altogether way too much for Flute to take in. So after a few stutters and attempts to describe what's going on, he just faints, hits the deck and then recovers. In the Globe, I did it every day for two weeks and I was a wee bit sore by the end of it, but it's actually quite a springy floor. I was able to do a proper tree-falling faint.

Bottom: Where are these lads?
             Where are these hearts?

Quince: Bottom!

Lines 21–22, 2008.

Why did the director have the other Mechanicals react like this when they realise Bottom has joined them?

Director's Note, 4.2

✔ The Mechanicals believe Bottom would have been a star; they cannot do the play without him.

✔ Bottom arrives and encourages them to prepare.

ACT 4 SCENE 2

Enter Quince, Flute, Snout, and Starveling.

Quince	Have you sent to Bottom's house? Is he come home yet?
Starveling	He cannot be heard of. Out of doubt he is transported.
Flute	If he come not, then the play is marred. It goes not forward, doth it?
Quince	It is not possible. You have not a man in all Athens able to discharge Pyramus but he.
Flute	No, he hath simply the best wit of any handicraft man in Athens.
Quince	Ye, and the best person too, and he is a very paramour for a sweet voice.
Flute	You must say "paragon". A paramour is (God bless us) a thing of naught.

Enter Snug.

Snug	Masters, the Duke is coming from the temple, and there is two or three lords and ladies more married. If our sport had gone forward, we had all been made men.
Flute	O sweet bully Bottom. Thus hath he lost sixpence a day during his life. He could not have 'scaped sixpence a day. And the Duke had not given him sixpence a day for playing Pyramus, I'll be hanged. He would have deserved it. Sixpence a day in Pyramus, or nothing.

Enter Bottom.

Bottom	Where are these lads? Where are these hearts?
Quince	Bottom! O most courageous day! O most happy hour!
Bottom	Masters, I am to discourse wonders, but ask me not what. For if I tell you, I am no true Athenian. I will tell you everything, right as it fell out.
Quince	Let us hear, sweet Bottom.
Bottom	Not a word of me. All that I will tell you is, that the Duke hath dined. Get your apparel together, good strings to your beards, new ribbons to your pumps, meet presently at the palace, every man look o'er his part. For the short and the long is, our play is preferred. In any case let Thisbe have clean linen, and let not him that plays the lion pare his nails, for they shall hang out for the lion's claws. And most dear actors, eat no onions nor garlic, for we are to utter sweet breath, and I do not doubt but to hear them say, it is a sweet comedy. No more words. Away! Go, away!

Exit all.

Line numbers and glosses:

2 **He cannot be heard of:** no one knows where he is
2 **Out of doubt:** certainly
2 **transported:** carried off or transformed
3 **marred:** spoiled
3–4 **It goes not forward, doth it?:** we can't put it on, can we?
6 **discharge:** play the part of

7 **wit:** intelligence

9 **person:** physical appearance
9 **paramour:** special lover, he means 'paragon' – a person who is an excellent example
12 **thing of naught:** a worthless person

15 **we had all been made men:** our fortunes would have been made
16–7 **sixpence a day during his life:** about half a day's wages for the rest of his life – the amount Flute thinks Theseus would have given as a reward for the play
17 **could not have 'scaped:** he was bound to get
18 **And:** and if
20 **in:** for
21 **hearts:** good friends
22 **courageous:** he probably means 'auspicious' – lucky
23 **discourse:** tell you
25 **right as it fell out:** just as it happened
27 **of:** out of
28 **apparel:** costumes
29 **strings:** to tie on false beards
29 **ribbons:** laces
29 **pumps:** light, indoor shoes
30 **presently:** straight away
30 **look o'er:** make sure he knows
31 **preferred:** on the short list

33 **pare:** cut

Emma Pallant
Hippolyta, 2012

I was dressed in a white, fairly masculine, suit and it was very modern – waving at the crowd, like a royal wedding, to signal that it's a celebration. It is a difficult transition from the beginning of the play when she is a spoil of war and 'fair Hippolyta'. He calls her by her name, which if you are a queen is a sort of demotion. But there's a lovely moment, I think, in the hunting scene. He calls her, in that scene, his queen, when there he is allowing her status again, which gives her a role and she feels that her position now has some power.

Hippolyta and Theseus, just after they have got married, 2012.

In this production, Theseus and Hippolyta entered like a couple during a modern royal wedding, coming out to show themselves to the crowd. Like a bride, Hippolyta holds a bouquet of flowers.
This photo of part of the audience in the yard was taken seconds after the main one. What has just happened?

Emma Pallant, Chook Sibtain

SHAKESPEARE'S WORLD

Cuts to the text

Lots of Shakespeare's plays survive in more than one version. Different versions were published during Shakespeare's lifetime, or soon after. There are three different texts for *A Midsummer Night's Dream*. The first was published in 1600, soon after the play was written. Another version appeared 19 years later, by which time Shakespeare was dead, and the third four years after that. The acting company had continued to perform the play, and the last version shows how performances changed over time. There are several cuts, so parts of the earlier text have disappeared. In this scene, the character Philostrate is replaced by Egeus, Hermia's father. One reason for this cut might be that Shakespeare's plays went on tour. Actors left the city to perform around the country. Tours were hard work and did not bring in as much money as shows in London. To keep profits up, fewer actors went on tour. Both are courtiers in Athens, and Philostrate's lines can easily be given to Egeus. One effect is that Egeus has to meet Lysander again, now Theseus has ruled Hermia can marry Lysander. This tension might be why the cut stayed in the play.

FROM THE REHEARSAL ROOM...

WHAT SHALL WE KEEP?

When putting on a production of a play, you often have to cut scenes or shorten them to maintain a reasonable playing time. The *Working Cuts* in this book are an example. In groups, take Act 5 Scene 1 from the beginning to line 106 and make an edit of the text, keeping about 40 lines.

- You should make sure that:
  - the story still makes sense
  - things stay in the same order
  - the humour of the scene is kept.
- Once you have finished, compare your edit with the one in the Script Machine in the online Dynamic Learning edition, or use the Playing Shakespeare site at http://2012.playing shakespeare.org/language/act-5-scene-1.

Enter Theseus, Hippolyta, with Philostrate and other lords and attendants.

Hippolyta   'Tis strange, my Theseus, that these lovers speak of.

Theseus   More strange than true. I never may believe
These antic fables, nor these fairy toys.
Lovers and madmen have such seething brains,
Such shaping fantasies, that apprehend   5
More than cool reason ever comprehends.
The lunatic, the lover and the poet
Are of imagination all compact.
One sees more devils than vast hell can hold,
That is the madman. The lover, all as frantic,   10
Sees Helen's beauty in a brow of Egypt.
The poet's eye, in a fine frenzy rolling,
Doth glance from heaven to earth, from earth to heaven.
And as imagination bodies forth
The forms of things unknown, the poet's pen   15
Turns them to shapes, and gives to airy nothing
A local habitation and a name.
Such tricks hath strong imagination,
That if it would but apprehend some joy,
It comprehends some bringer of that joy.   20
Or in the night, imagining some fear,
How easy is a bush supposed a bear?

Hippolyta   But all the story of the night told over,
And all their minds transfigured so together,
More witnesseth than fancy's images   25
And grows to something of great constancy.
But howsoever, strange and admirable.

Enter Lysander, Demetrius, Hermia and Helena.

Theseus   Here come the lovers, full of joy and mirth. —
Joy, gentle friends, joy and fresh days of love
Accompany your hearts.

Lysander   More than to us   30
Wait in your royal walks, your board, your bed.

Theseus   Come now, what masques, what dances shall we have,
To wear away this long age of three hours
Between our after-supper and bedtime?
Where is our usual manager of mirth?   35
What revels are in hand? Is there no play
To ease the anguish of a torturing hour?
Call Philostrate.

Philostrate   Here, mighty Theseus.

Theseus   Say, what abridgement have you for this evening?
What masque? What music? How shall we beguile   40
The lazy time if not with some delight?

1   **that:** the things
3   **antic fables:** bizarre stories
3   **fairy toys:** childish stories about fairies
4   **seething:** churning
5   **shaping fantasies:** inventive imaginations
5   **apprehend:** seem to understand
8   **Are of imagination all compact:** are made up entirely by imagination
11   **Helen:** Helen of Troy (famously beautiful)
11   **in a brow of Egypt:** in a dark complexion (seen as less attractive than a fair one); also a reference to Cleopatra, famously beautiful queen of Egypt
14   **bodies forth:** produces
15   **forms:** shapes
16   **Turns them to shapes:** brings them to life
17   **A local habitation and a name:** a solid reality
19   **if it would but apprehend:** it only has to think of
20   **It comprehends some bringer:** to imagine someone who will bring
24   **transfigured:** changed
24   **together:** in the same way
25   **More witnesseth:** is evidence of more
25   **fancy's images:** imagined events
26   **constancy:** reliability
27   **howsoever:** in any case
27   **admirable:** extraordinary

31   **board:** dining table

32   **masques:** entertainments with dancing and music

39   **abridgement:** pastime to fill the time

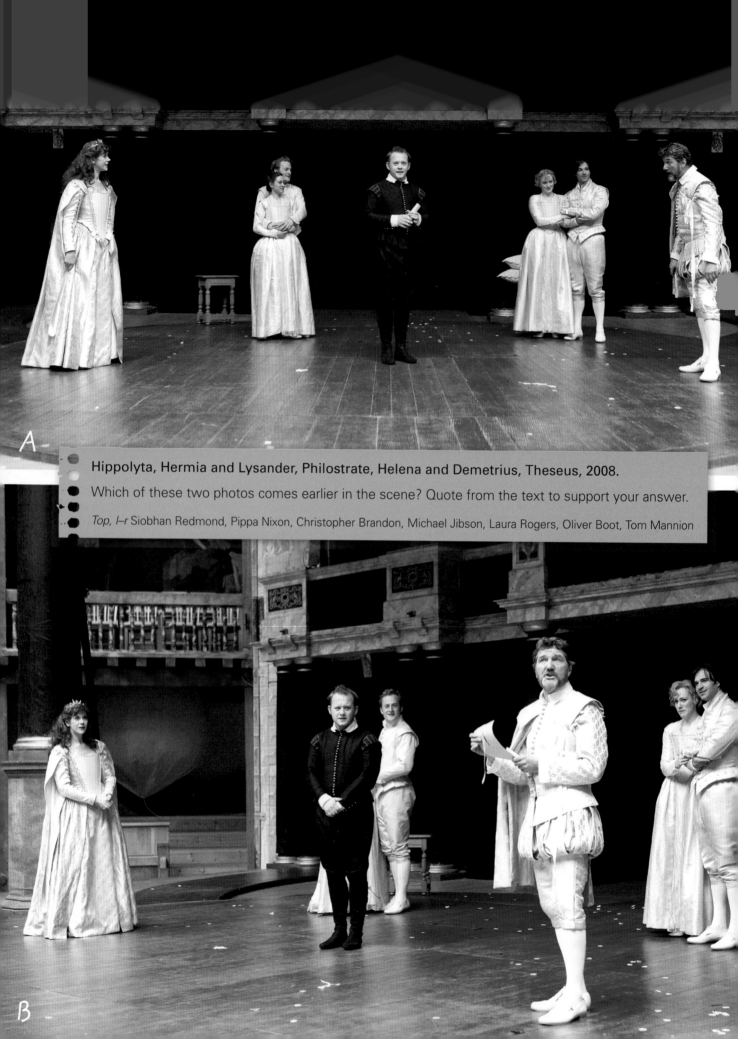

A

Hippolyta, Hermia and Lysander, Philostrate, Helena and Demetrius, Theseus, 2008.

Which of these two photos comes earlier in the scene? Quote from the text to support your answer.

Top, l–r Siobhan Redmond, Pippa Nixon, Christopher Brandon, Michael Jibson, Laura Rogers, Oliver Boot, Tom Mannion

B

Philostrate	*[Handing Theseus a piece of paper.]*	
	There is a brief how many sports are ripe.	
	Make choice of which your Highness will see first.	
Theseus	*[Reading.]* The battle with the Centaurs, to be sung	
	By an Athenian eunuch to the harp.	45
	We'll none of that. That have I told my love	
	In glory of my kinsman Hercules.	
	[Reading.] The riot of the tipsy Bacchanals,	
	Tearing the Thracian singer in their rage.	
	That is an old device, and it was played	50
	When I from Thebes came last a conqueror.	
	[Reading.] The thrice three Muses, mourning for the death	
	Of Learning, late deceased in beggary.	
	That is some satire, keen and critical,	
	Not sorting with a nuptial ceremony.	55
	[Reading.] A tedious brief scene of young Pyramus	
	And his love Thisbe. Very tragical mirth.	
	Merry and tragical? Tedious and brief?	
	That is, hot ice and wondrous strange snow.	
	How shall we find the concord of this discord?	60
Philostrate	A play there is, my lord, some ten words long,	
	Which is as brief as I have known a play,	
	But by ten words, my lord, it is too long,	
	Which makes it tedious, for in all the play	
	There is not one word apt, one player fitted.	65
	And tragical, my noble lord, it is,	
	For Pyramus therein doth kill himself.	
	Which when I saw rehearsed, I must confess,	
	Made mine eyes water, but more merry tears	
	The passion of loud laughter never shed.	70
Theseus	What are they that do play it?	
Philostrate	Hard-handed men that work in Athens here,	
	Which never laboured in their minds till now,	
	And now have toiled their unbreathed memories	
	With this same play, against your nuptial.	75
Theseus	And we will hear it.	
Philostrate	No, my noble lord,	
	It is not for you. I have heard it over,	
	And it is nothing, nothing in the world,	
	Unless you can find sport in their intents,	
	Extremely stretched and conned with cruel pain,	80
	To do you service.	
Theseus	I will hear that play.	
	For never anything can be amiss,	
	When simpleness and duty tender it.	
	Go bring them in — and take your places, ladies.	
	[Exit Philostrate.]	
Hippolyta	I love not to see wretchedness o'erchargèd,	85
	And duty in his service perishing.	

Glossary

42 **brief:** summary
42 **sports:** entertainments
42 **ripe:** ready for performance

47 **In glory of:** to show off the deeds of

50 **device:** entertainment

54 **keen:** sharp-tongued
55 **sorting with:** appropriate for

59 **That is:** that's like saying
60 **concord:** agreement
60 **discord:** disagreement

65 **fitted:** suitable for his part

74 **toiled:** overworked
74 **unbreathed:** inexperienced
75 **against:** to be ready for

79 **intents:** attempts
80 **conned:** learned
82 **never anything can be amiss:** nothing can ever be wrong

83 **simpleness:** innocence
83 **tender:** offer

85 **wretchedness o'ercharged:** humble people stretched beyond their limit
86 **perishing:** failing

Quince starts the Prologue of the Mechanicals' play, 2008.

Shakespeare gives his actors and directors a challenge here. A play within a play is being performed, and there is an audience for that play, then there is the real audience watching both.

1 How did the director of the 2008 production solve this staging problem?

2 Look back at the description of the original Globe Theatre stage (pages 2–3). How else could this be staged using the features of original Globe theatre?

SHAKESPEARE'S WORLD

Performing at the royal court

For most of the year, Shakespeare's company made a profit by playing to the public. Sometimes, though, they were invited to give performances for Queen Elizabeth at her court. These made much more money than their regular shows. They also made the company more famous. A court performance differed from one at the Globe in many ways: the audience was special; performances were indoors; and there was better music with more musicians. As at the Globe, both the audience and the actors were in the light. This meant that the actors would be able to see the queen whilst they were on stage. Some plays written for court have a Chorus or Prologue speak to the queen directly. Shakespeare's plays probably did, but such speeches are lost.

SHAKESPEARE'S WORLD

Dumb shows

In this speech, Quince, in the part of Prologue, introduces the characters of *Pyramus and Thisbe*. He also tells the entire story of the play, even the ending. It was a famous story, so the audience would have known it anyway. However, audiences in Elizabethan England seem not to have valued suspense in a story in the way that we do. What they did enjoy was the particular way in which a play presented that story. A dumb show is the term for actors telling a story in mime. They go through all of the action of the play, but stay silent. That way, when the play really starts, the audience can concentrate on the poetry. This is probably what happened in *A Midsummer Night's Dream*: Bottom, Flute and the rest performed their actions whilst Quince was talking.

Theseus	Why gentle sweet, you shall see no such thing.	
Hippolyta	He says they can do nothing in this kind.	
Theseus	The kinder we, to give them thanks for nothing.	
	Our sport shall be to take what they mistake, 90	
	And what poor duty cannot do, noble respect	
	Takes it in might, not merit.	
	Where I have come, great clerks have purposèd	
	To greet me with premeditated welcomes.	
	Where I have seen them shiver and look pale, 95	
	Make periods in the midst of sentences,	
	Throttle their practised accent in their fears	
	And, in conclusion, dumbly have broke off	
	Not paying me a welcome. Trust me, sweet,	
	Out of this silence yet I picked a welcome. 100	
	And in the modesty of fearful duty	
	I read as much as from the rattling tongue	
	Of saucy and audacious eloquence.	
	Love, therefore, and tongue-tied simplicity	
	In least, speak most to my capacity. 105	

[Enter Philostrate.]

Philostrate	So please your grace, the Prologue is addressed.	
Theseus	Let him approach.	

Trumpets sound offstage.
Enter Quince as the Prologue.

Prologue (Quince)	*If we offend, it is with our good will.*	
	That you should think, we come not to offend,	
	But with good will. To show our simple skill, 110	
	That is the true beginning of our end.	
	Consider then, we come but in despite.	
	We do not come, as minding to content you,	
	Our true intent is. All for your delight,	
	We are not here. That you should here repent you, 115	
	The actors are at hand, and, by their show,	
	You shall know all, that you are like to know.	

Theseus	This fellow doth not stand upon points.	
Lysander	He hath rid his prologue like a rough colt. He knows	
	not the stop. A good moral, my lord. It is not enough to 120	
	speak, but to speak true.	
Hippolyta	Indeed he hath played on his prologue like a child on a	
	recorder, a sound, but not in government.	
Theseus	His speech was like a tangled chain, nothing impaired,	
	but all disordered. Who is next? 125	

Enter a trumpeter, followed by Bottom as Pyramus,
Flute as Thisbe, Snout as Wall, Starveling as Moonshine,
and Snug as the Lion.

Prologue (Quince)	*Gentles, perchance you wonder at this show,*	
	But wonder on, till truth make all things plain.	
	This man is Pyramus, if you would know.	

Glossary notes:

88 **He:** Philostrate
88 **in this kind:** of this sort
90 **sport:** entertainment
90 **take:** accept
91 **noble respect:** our generous attitude
92 **in might, not merit:** as what it is intended to be, not how it turns out
93 **clerks:** scholars
94 **premeditated welcomes:** carefully planned speeches
96 **Make periods:** stop talking
97 **Throttle:** choke
97 **accent:** patterns of speech
100 **picked:** found
103 **saucy:** presumptious
103 **audacious:** over-confident
103 **eloquence:** well-thought-out speeches
105 **In least:** by doing less
105 **to my capacity:** as I see it
106 **addressed:** ready
108–9 ***good will. That:*** a misplaced full stop mangles the sense. This happens several times in the play of *Pyramus and Thisbe*
111 ***our end:*** our aim
112 ***in despite:*** maliciously
113 ***as minding:*** intending
115 ***repent you:*** regret your choice
118 **stand upon points:** bother about details (here referring to punctuation)
119 **rid:** ridden
119 **rough colt:** untrained young horse
120 **the stop:** full stops
121 **true:** double meaning: 1) the truth; 2) correctly
123 **not in government:** out of control
124 **nothing impaired:** not damaged
126 ***Gentles:*** ladies and gentlemen
126 ***perchance:*** maybe

FROM THE REHEARSAL ROOM...

MIME — THE DUMB SHOW

In groups of six, read through the Prologue (lines 126–150), then cast Quince and the rest of the characters mentioned.

- Make a note of the entrances and exits of the characters, what we are told they do, as well as any descriptions of what they might be like.

- Now, taking your notes into consideration, make a mime to show the story while Quince speaks the lines. Give your mime a genre. For example: a melodrama, a soap opera, a cartoon, or a horror story.

- Share your mime with the other groups.

1 What genre best fits the language used and the story? Give reasons for your answer.

2 Why do you think Shakespeare has this dumb show at this particular moment in the play?

3 What effect does it have?

Thisbe, Wall, and Pyramus with Theseus and Hippolyta in the foreground, 2002.

1 How did each production stage the Wall?

2 Which line do you think was being spoken when each photo was taken? Give reasons for your answer.

A Paul Hunter, Jonathan Bond, Sam Parks, Peter Bankolé

B Aled Pugh, Patrick Lennox, John Ramm

This beauteous lady, Thisbe is certain.
This man, with lime and rough-cast, doth present   130
Wall, that vile Wall which did these lovers sunder.
And through Wall's chink (poor souls) they are content
To whisper. At the which, let no man wonder.
This man, with lantern, dog, and bush of thorn,
Presenteth Moonshine. For if you will know,   135
By moonshine did these lovers think no scorn
To meet at Ninus' tomb, there, there to woo.
This grisly beast (which Lion hight by name)
The trusty Thisbe, coming first by night,
Did scare away, or rather did affright.   140
And as she fled, her mantle she did fall;
Which Lion vile with bloody mouth did stain.
Anon comes Pyramus, sweet youth and tall,
And finds his trusty Thisbe's mantle slain;
Whereat, with blade, with bloody blameful blade,   145
He bravely broached his boiling bloody breast,
And Thisbe, tarrying in mulberry shade,
His dagger drew, and died. For all the rest,
Let Lion, Moonshine, Wall, and lovers twain,
At large discourse, while here they do remain.   150

Exit Quince as Prologue, Bottom as Pyramus, Flute as
Thisbe, Starveling as Moonshine, and Snug as the Lion.

Theseus	I wonder if the lion be to speak.
Demetrius	No wonder, my lord. One lion may, when many asses do.
Wall (Snout)	*In this same interlude, it doth befall,*
	That I, one Snout (by name) present a wall.
	And such a wall, as I would have you think, 155
	That had in it a crannied hole or chink,
	Through which the lovers, Pyramus and Thisbe
	Did whisper often, very secretly.
	This loam, this rough-cast, and this stone doth show,
	That I am that same wall, the truth is so. 160
	And this the cranny is, right and sinister,
	Through which the fearful lovers are to whisper.
Theseus	Would you desire lime and hair to speak better?
Demetrius	It is the wittiest partition that ever I heard discourse, my lord. 165

Enter Bottom as Pyramus.

Theseus	Pyramus draws near the wall. Silence.
Pyramus (Bottom)	*O grim-looked night, O night with hue so black,*
	O night, which ever art, when day is not.
	O night, O night, alack, alack, alack,
	I fear my Thisbe's promise is forgot. 170
	And thou, O wall, O sweet, O lovely wall,
	That stand'st between her father's ground and mine.
	Thou wall, O wall, O sweet and lovely wall,
	Show me thy chink, to blink through with mine eyne.

Glossary

131 **sunder:** divide, keep apart

135 **Presenteth:** represents
135 **if you will know:** you need to know
136 **think no scorn:** see as no disgrace
138 **grisly:** terrifying
138 **hight:** is called
141 **mantle:** cloak
141 **she did fall:** she dropped
143 **Anon:** instantly
143 **tall:** brave

145 **Whereat:** on seeing this
146 **broached:** stabbed
147 **tarrying:** waiting
147 **mulberry shade:** the shadow of a mulberry tree
149 **lovers twain:** the two lovers
150 **At large discourse:** tell the story at length

152 **No wonder:** It wouldn't surprise me
153 **interlude:** short play
156 **crannied hole:** *Pyramus and Thisbe* is full of puns on 'hole' and the idea of a vagina or anus

161 **sinister:** left

164 **partition:** dividing wall

167 **hue:** colour
168 **art:** is
169 **alack:** an expression of misery

172 **ground:** land

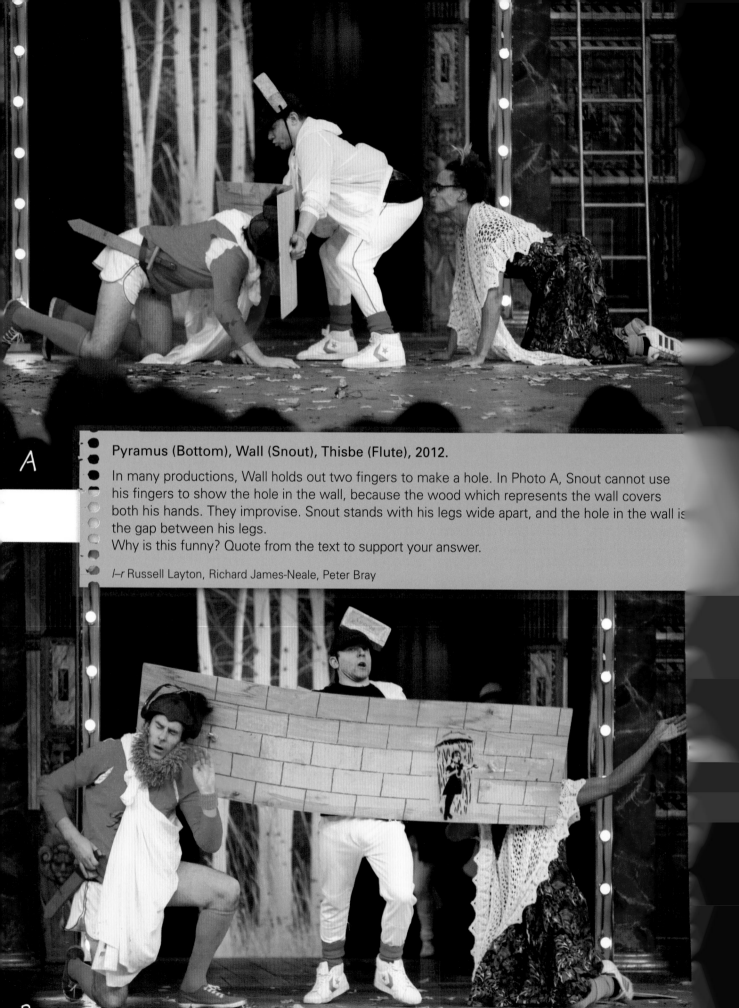

A

Pyramus (Bottom), Wall (Snout), Thisbe (Flute), 2012.

In many productions, Wall holds out two fingers to make a hole. In Photo A, Snout cannot use his fingers to show the hole in the wall, because the wood which represents the wall covers both his hands. They improvise. Snout stands with his legs wide apart, and the hole in the wall is the gap between his legs.

Why is this funny? Quote from the text to support your answer.

l–r Russell Layton, Richard James-Neale, Peter Bray

B

	Thanks, courteous wall. Jove shield thee well for this. 175
	[Kneeling, facing Wall.]
	But what see I? No Thisbe do I see.
	O wicked wall, through whom I see no bliss,
	Cursed be thy stones for thus deceiving me.
Theseus	The wall methinks being sensible, should curse again.
Bottom	No, in truth sir, he should not. *Deceiving me* is Thisbe's 180 cue. She is to enter now, and I am to spy her through the wall. You shall see, it will fall pat as I told you.
	Enter Flute as Thisbe.
	Yonder she comes.
Thisbe (Flute)	*O wall, full often hast thou heard my moans,*
	For parting my fair Pyramus, and me. 185
	My cherry lips have often kissed thy stones,
	Thy stones with lime and hair knit up in thee.
Pyramus (Bottom)	*I see a voice. Now will I to the chink,*
	To spy and I can hear my Thisbe's face.
	Thisbe?
Thisbe (Flute)	*My love? Thou art my love I think.* 190
Pyramus (Bottom)	*Think what thou wilt, I am thy lover's grace,*
	And like Limander am I trusty still.
Thisbe (Flute)	*And I like Helen, till the Fates me kill.*
Pyramus (Bottom)	*Not Shafalus to Procrus was so true.*
Thisbe (Flute)	*As Shafalus to Procrus, I to you.* 195
Pyramus (Bottom)	*O kiss me through the hole of this vile wall.*
Thisbe (Flute)	*[Kneeling to kiss him through the Wall.]*
	I kiss the wall's hole, not your lips at all.
Pyramus (Bottom)	*Wilt thou at Ninny's tomb meet me straightway?*
Thisbe (Flute)	*'Tide life, 'tide death, I come without delay.*
	[Exit Pyramus (Bottom) and Thisbe (Flute) in different directions.]
Wall (Snout)	*Thus have I, Wall, my part dischargèd so,* 200
	And being done, thus Wall away doth go.
	Exit Snout as Wall.
Theseus	Now is the mural down between the two neighbours.
Demetrius	No remedy my lord, when walls are so wilful to hear without warning.
Hippolyta	This is the silliest stuff that ever I heard. 205
Theseus	The best in this kind are but shadows, and the worst are no worse, if imagination amend them.
Hippolyta	It must be your imagination then, and not theirs.

175 *Jove:* king of the gods in Roman myths

178 *stones: Pyramus and Thisbe* has puns on 'stones', another word for 'testicles'

179 **sensible:** able to have feelings
179 **again:** in return

182 **fall pat:** work out exactly

183 **Yonder:** there

189 *and:* if

192 *Limander:* he means 'Leander' – a famous lover
192 *trusty:* faithful
193 *Helen:* he means 'Hero' – Leander's lover
194 *Shafalus ... Procrus:* he means 'Cephalus' and 'Procris' – famously faithful

199 *'Tide:* come

202 **mural:** wall

203-4 **walls are so wilful ... warning:** playing with the proverb 'walls have ears'

206 **in this kind:** of this sort
206 **shadows:** double meaning: 1) reflections of reality; 2) actors
207 **amend:** improve

Theseus and Demetrius watch Snug as the Lion, with other members of the Mechanicals' play cast in the background, 2008.

1 Pick a line or lines from the text which would make a good caption for this photo.

2 Explain why you think it is a good fit.

Tom Mannion, Oliver Boot, Robert Goodale

Actor's view

Louise Collins
Snug/Lion, 2012

He really wants to do a good job and he really wants to try. But he comes from a place of earnestness and fear. So he is scared of getting things wrong, but he is going to try his best. He has never been on stage before. When he goes on for the first time in the Prologue he gets so struck with stage fright that he doesn't think he can go back on, and when he plucks up the courage and goes on and says 'lion' – the joy and the thrill that he's done it. He gets carried away and says it again as he can't stop. He is just in that moment of 'I am a lion, this is just amazing'.

SHAKESPEARE'S WORLD

Who was Shakespeare making fun of?

When the acting companies of Shakespeare's time went on tour, they performed in two main venues. Some of the time they performed in towns, and sometimes they gave 'private' performances in the great houses of the nobility. These performances would be similar to the performances at the royal court (see page 94). The performances would be indoors – usually in the afternoon – to take advantage of daylight, perhaps helped by candles.

In this scene Shakespeare seems to be making fun of a number of targets. The Mechanicals' play allows him to make fun of amateur actors. In Bottom's desire to dominate everything, he may also be making fun of some of his fellow professionals. He could also be making fun of his aristocratic audiences. During the play Theseus, Hippolyta and the lovers often interrupt, sometimes clearly upsetting the actors. Perhaps Shakespeare and his fellow actors remembered rude audiences they had performed for when they were playing this scene.

Theseus	If we imagine no worse of them than they of themselves, they may pass for excellent men. 210
	Enter Snug as Lion and Starveling as Moonshine.
	Here come two noble beasts in, a man and a lion.
Lion (Snug)	*You, ladies, you (whose gentle hearts do fear*
	The smallest monstrous mouse that creeps on floor),
	May now perchance both quake and tremble here,
	When lion rough in wildest rage doth roar. 215
	Then know that I, one Snug the joiner am
	A lion fell, nor else no lion's dam.
	For, if I should as lion come in strife
	Into this place, 'twere pity on my life.
Theseus	A very gentle beast, and of a good conscience. 220
Demetrius	The very best at a beast, my lord, that e'er I saw.
Lysander	This lion is a very fox for his valour.
Theseus	True, and a goose for his discretion.
Lysander	Not so my lord, for his valour cannot carry his discretion, and the fox carries the goose. 225
Theseus	His discretion, I am sure, cannot carry his valour, for the goose carries not the fox. It is well. Leave it to his discretion, and let us listen to the Moon.
Moon (Starveling)	*This lanthorn doth the hornèd moon present.* —
Demetrius	He should have worn the horns on his head. 230
Theseus	He is no crescent, and his horns are invisible within the circumference.
Moon (Starveling)	*This lanthorn doth the hornèd moon present.*
	Myself the man i' the moon do seem to be. —
Theseus	This is the greatest error of all the rest. The man should 235 be put into the lanthorn. How is it else the man i' the moon?
Demetrius	He dares not come there for the candle. For, you see, it is already in snuff.
Hippolyta	I am aweary of this moon. Would he would change! 240
Theseus	It appears, by his small light of discretion, that he is in the wane. But yet in courtesy, in all reason, we must stay the time.
Lysander	Proceed Moon.
Starveling	All that I have to say, is, to tell you that the lanthorn is 245 the moon, I, the man in the moon, this thorn-bush my thorn-bush, and this dog, my dog.
Demetrius	Why, all these should be in the lanthorn, for all these are in the moon. *[Enter Thisbe.]*
	But silence, here comes Thisbe. 250

217 *fell*: fierce
217 *nor else*: in no way
217 *dam*: mother
218 *in strife*: to be violent
219 *'twere pity on my life*: double meaning: 1) I'd feel terrible; 2) my life would be in danger
220 **of a good conscience**: very considerate
221 **at a beast**: at playing a beast
222 **a very fox**: cunning
222 **valour**: physical courage
223 **a goose**: silly
225 **discretion**: judgement
230 **horns on his head**: the horns of a cuckold whose wife is unfaithful
231 **no crescent**: isn't fat (he's Starveling)
233 *doth the*: because of the
239 **in snuff**: double meaning: 1) in need of blowing out; 2) offended
242 **in courtesy**: out of politeness
242 **in all reason**: it's only reasonable
243 **stay the time**: sit it out

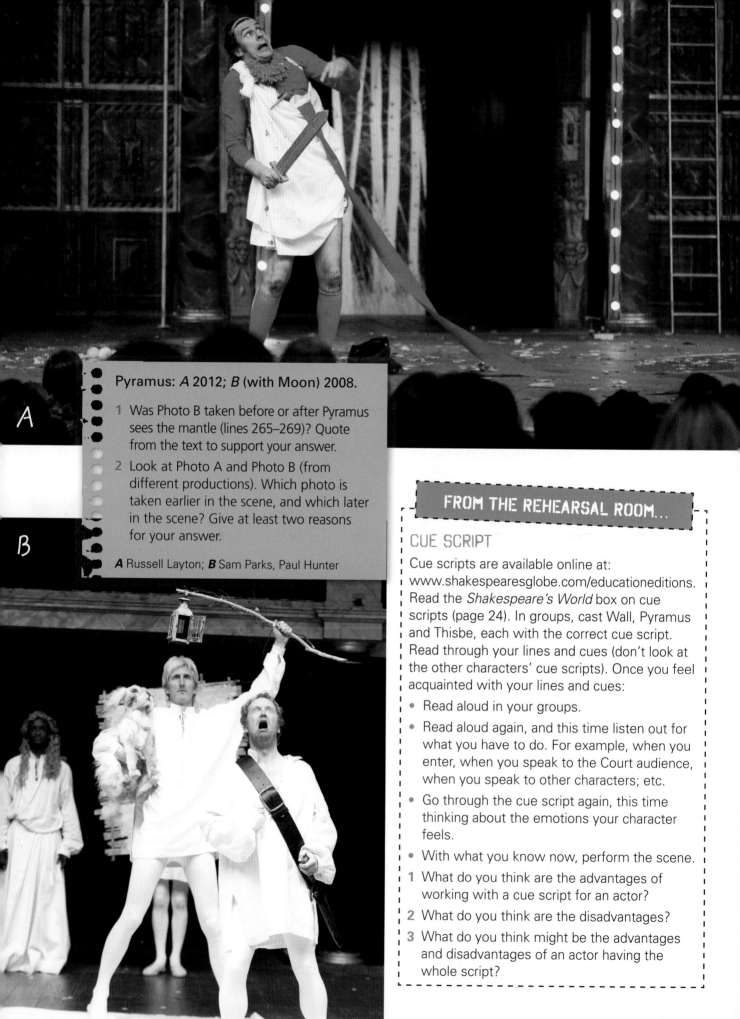

A

B

Pyramus: *A* 2012; *B* (with Moon) 2008.

1 Was Photo B taken before or after Pyramus sees the mantle (lines 265–269)? Quote from the text to support your answer.

2 Look at Photo A and Photo B (from different productions). Which photo is taken earlier in the scene, and which later in the scene? Give at least two reasons for your answer.

A Russell Layton; *B* Sam Parks, Paul Hunter

FROM THE REHEARSAL ROOM...

CUE SCRIPT

Cue scripts are available online at: www.shakespearesglobe.com/educationeditions. Read the *Shakespeare's World* box on cue scripts (page 24). In groups, cast Wall, Pyramus and Thisbe, each with the correct cue script. Read through your lines and cues (don't look at the other characters' cue scripts). Once you feel acquainted with your lines and cues:

- Read aloud in your groups.

- Read aloud again, and this time listen out for what you have to do. For example, when you enter, when you speak to the Court audience, when you speak to other characters; etc.

- Go through the cue script again, this time thinking about the emotions your character feels.

- With what you know now, perform the scene.

1 What do you think are the advantages of working with a cue script for an actor?

2 What do you think are the disadvantages?

3 What do you think might be the advantages and disadvantages of an actor having the whole script?

Thisbe (Flute)	*This is old Ninny's tomb. Where is my love?*
Snug (Lion)	*O —*

The Lion roars. Thisbe drops her mantle and runs off.

Demetrius	Well roared, Lion.
Theseus	Well run, Thisbe.
Hippolyta	Well shone Moon. Truly, the Moon shines with a good 255 grace.

[Snug, as the Lion shakes Thisbe's mantle, then exits.]

Theseus	Well moused, Lion.

257   **moused:** shaken (Thisbe's cloak)

Enter Bottom as Pyramus.

Demetrius	And then came Pyramus.
Lysander	And so the lion vanished.

**Pyramus
(Bottom)**
	Sweet Moon, I thank thee for thy sunny beams, 260
	I thank thee, Moon, for shining now so bright;
	For by thy gracious, golden, glittering beams,
	I trust to take of truest Thisbe sight.
	But stay, O spite! But mark, poor knight,
	   What dreadful dole is here? 265
	Eyes, do you see! How can it be!
	   O dainty duck! O dear!
	Thy mantle good, what, stained with blood!
	   Approach, ye Furies fell!
	O Fates! Come, come, cut thread and thrum, 270
	   Quail, crush, conclude, and quell.

265   ***dole:*** misery

269   ***Furies:*** three goddesses of vengeance in Roman and Greek myth

270   ***Fates:*** three women in the myths of many cultures who controlled human life

270   ***cut thread:*** the Fates cut the threads of people's lives to kill them

270   ***thrum:*** the ends of the threads in a piece of weaving left on the loom when the cloth is cut off

271   ***Quail:*** make life waste away

271   ***quell:*** kill

Theseus	This passion, and the death of a dear friend, would go near to make a man look sad.
Hippolyta	Beshrew my heart, but I pity the man.

**Pyramus
(Bottom)**
	O wherefore, Nature, didst thou lions frame? 275
	Since lion vile hath here deflowered my dear.
	Which is — no, no — which was the fairest dame
	That lived, that loved, that liked, that looked with cheer.
	Come tears, confound. Out sword, and wound
	   The pap of Pyramus.
	Ay, that left pap, where heart doth hop.
	   [Stabbing himself.] *Thus die I, thus, thus, thus.*
	Now am I dead, now am I fled,
	   My soul is in the sky.
	Tongue, lose thy light, Moon take thy flight, *[Exit Starveling.]* 285
	   Now die, die, die, die, die. *[He dies.]*

272   **passion:** fit of grief

272   **friend:** could be used to mean 'lover'

274   **Beshrew:** curse

275   ***frame:*** create

276   ***deflowered:*** taken the virginity of – he means 'devoured'

278   ***looked with cheer:*** smiled

280   ***pap:*** breast

285   ***Tongue:*** he means 'eye'

Demetrius	No die, but an ace for him, for he is but one.
Lysander	Less than an ace, man. For he is dead, he is nothing.
Theseus	With the help of a surgeon he might yet recover, and prove an ass. 290
Hippolyta	How chance Moonshine is gone before Thisbe comes

287   **die:** he is referring to dice (which have many spots)

287   **an ace:** single spot on a dice

287   **he is but one:** there's only one of him

290   **prove:** turn out to be

290   **ass:** pun on 'ace'

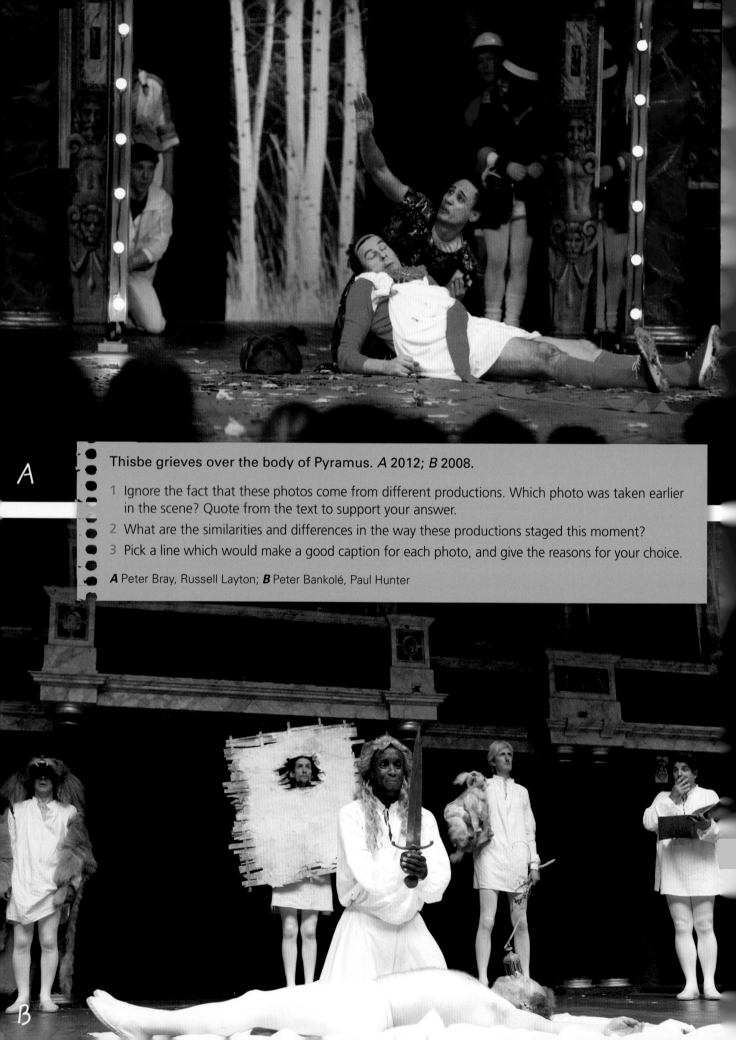

A

Thisbe grieves over the body of Pyramus. *A* 2012; *B* 2008.

1 Ignore the fact that these photos come from different productions. Which photo was taken earlier in the scene? Quote from the text to support your answer.

2 What are the similarities and differences in the way these productions staged this moment?

3 Pick a line which would make a good caption for each photo, and give the reasons for your choice.

A Peter Bray, Russell Layton; *B* Peter Bankolé, Paul Hunter

B

back and finds her lover?

Enter Flute as Thisbe.

Theseus	She will find him by starlight. Here she comes and her passion ends the play.	
Hippolyta	Methinks she should not use a long one for such a Pyramus. I hope she will be brief.	295
Demetrius	A moth will turn the balance, which Pyramus, which Thisbe, is the better. He for a man, God warrant us; she for a woman, God bless us.	
Lysander	She hath spied him already with those sweet eyes.	300
Demetrius	And thus she means, videlicet —	

Thisbe (Flute)

Asleep my love? What, dead, my dove?
    O Pyramus arise!
Speak, speak. Quite dumb? Dead, dead? A tomb
    Must cover thy sweet eyes.   305
These lily lips, This cherry nose,
    These yellow cowslip cheeks
Are gone, are gone. Lovers make moan.
    His eyes were green as leeks.
O Sisters Three, come, come to me,   310
    With hands as pale as milk,
Lay them in gore, since you have shore
    With shears, his thread of silk.
Tongue, not a word. Come, trusty sword,
    Come blade, my breast imbrue.   315
And farewell friends,   [Stabbing herself.]   *thus Thisbe ends.*
    Adieu, adieu, adieu.

Theseus	Moonshine and Lion are left to bury the dead.	
Demetrius	Ay, and Wall too.	
Bottom	[Starting up.] No, I assure you, the wall is down that parted their fathers. Will it please you to see the Epilogue, or to hear a Bergomask dance between two of our company?	320
Theseus	No Epilogue, I pray you, for your play needs no excuse. Never excuse. For when the players are all dead, there need none to be blamed. Marry, if he that writ it had played Pyramus, and hanged himself in Thisbe's garter, it would have been a fine tragedy. And so it is, truly, and very notably discharged.	325
	But come, your Bergomask. Let your Epilogue alone.	330

[Enter Quince, Snout, Snug and Starveling; they are joined by Bottom and Flute. Two of them dance.]

The iron tongue of midnight hath told twelve.
Lovers, to bed, 'tis almost fairy time.
I fear we shall outsleep the coming morn,
As much as we this night have overwatched.
This palpable gross play hath well beguiled   335

---

298 **warrant:** save

301 **videlicet:** Latin: 'that is to say'

310 ***Sisters Three:*** the Fates

312 ***gore:*** blood
312 ***shore:*** cut

315 ***imbrue:*** stab

322 **Bergomask dance:** a comic country dance
322 **between:** performed by

326 **Marry:** 'by the Virgin Mary', used at the start of a sentence for emphasis as 'well' is now
327 **garter:** a band to hold up a woman's stocking
329 **very notably discharged:** a remarkable performance

331 **iron tongue:** clapper of a bell
331 **told:** counted
334 **As much as:** due to the fact that
334 **overwatched:** stayed up too long
335 **palpable gross:** obviously clumsy
335 **beguiled:** magicked away

A Puck, 2008.

After the performance is over, the stage management team manually sweep the stage. Here the director has given Puck a broom for his speech (lines 339–358).

1 Part of the reason is that the Mechanicals' play has just finished. What is the other reason for giving him a broom?

Michael Jibson

B The stage as Oberon sang 'Shall upon their children be', 2008.

2 What are the differences between how the song was staged in this production, and the way it is in the text?

3 Why might the director have made these changes?

The heavy gait of night. Sweet friends, to bed.
A fortnight hold we this solemnity,
In nightly revels and new jollity.

Exit all.

Enter Puck.

Puck   Now the hungry lion roars,
And the wolf beholds the moon,   340
Whilst the heavy ploughman snores,
All with weary task fordone.
Now the wasted brands do glow,
Whilst the screech-owl, screeching loud,
Puts the wretch that lies in woe   345
In remembrance of a shroud.
Now it is the time of night,
That the graves, all gaping wide,
Every one lets forth his sprite,
In the church-way paths to glide.   350
And we fairies, that do run
By the triple Hecate's team,
From the presence of the sun,
Following darkness like a dream,
Now are frolic; Not a mouse   355
Shall disturb this hallowed house,
I am sent with broom before,
To sweep the dust behind the door.

Enter Oberon and Titania, with all their followers.

Oberon   Through the house give glimmering light,
By the dead and drowsy fire,   360
Every elf and fairy sprite,
Hop as light as bird from briar,
And this ditty after me,
Sing and dance it trippingly.

Titania   First rehearse this song by rote,   365
To each word a warbling note.
Hand in hand, with fairy grace,
Will we sing, and bless this place.

[Oberon leads the fairies in a song and dance.]

All   *Now, until the break of day,*
Through this house each fairy stray.   370
To the best bride-bed will we,
Which by us shall blessèd be.
And the issue there create
Ever shall be fortunate.
So shall all the couples three   375
Ever true in loving be,
And the blots of Nature's hand
Shall not in their issue stand.
Never mole, hare-lip, nor scar,
Nor mark prodigious, such as are   380
Despisèd in nativity,
Shall upon their children be.

336 **heavy gait:** slow progress
337 **solemnity:** celebration

341 **heavy:** exhausted
342 **weary task:** tiring jobs
342 **fordone:** worn out
343 **wasted brands:** burnt logs

345 **wretch:** fearful person
346 **shroud:** the cloth dead people were wrapped in to be buried

349 **sprite:** spirit
352 **triple Hecate:** Greek and Roman goddess of witchcraft and the night who lives in Heaven, on Earth and in the Underworld
352 **team:** the dragons who pulled her chariot
355 **Now are frolic:** now can play

357 **before:** before everyone else

363 **ditty:** song
364 **trippingly:** lightly

365 **rehearse:** learn
365 **by rote:** off by heart

371 **best:** most important

373 **issue:** children
373 **create:** created

377 **the blots of Nature's hand:** birth defects
378 **stand:** exist
379 **hare-lip:** split lip
380 **prodigious:** unlucky
381 **Despisèd in nativity:** seen as the mark of unlucky babies

107

Puck, just about to say 'If we shadows have offended', line 392, 2012.

This production cut everything from the dance (after line 331) to this Epilogue (a speech to end the play). While the dance was happening, Puck came up though a trapdoor in the stage, and blew his whistle. At this, all the dancers froze, and Puck walked amongst them saying the Epilogue.

1 How does this show the difference between the magical world and the real world in the play?

l–r Richard James-Neale, Carlyss Peer, Russell Layton, Fergal McElherron, Louise Collins, William Oxborrow, Peter Bray

Director's Note, 5.1

✔ Theseus decides they should see the Mechanicals' play, and they do (although they sometimes interrupt it).
✔ After the play, the Mechanicals do a dance, and then the newly married couples go to bed.
✔ Puck, Oberon, Titania and the fairies end the play with a song and dance.
✔ Did the newly married couples enjoy the play?

With this field-dew consecrate,
Every fairy take his gait,
And each several chamber bless. 385
Through this palace with sweet peace;
And the owner of it blessed
Ever shall in safety rest.
Trip away, make no stay,
Meet me all by break of day. 390

Exit all except Puck.

Puck   If we shadows have offended,
Think but this, and all is mended,
That you have but slumbered here,
While these visions did appear.
And this weak and idle theme, 395
No more yielding but a dream,
Gentles, do not reprehend.
If you pardon, we will mend.
And as I am an honest Puck,
If we have unearnèd luck 400
Now to 'scape the serpent's tongue,
We will make amends ere long.
Else the Puck a liar call.
So good night unto you all.
Give me your hands, if we be friends, 405
And Robin shall restore amends.   *Exit.*

383 **consecrate:** blessed
384 **take his gait:** go his own way
385 **each several chamber:** every single room

389 **make no stay:** don't dawdle

391 **shadows:** double meaning: 1) fairies; 2) actors
392 **mended:** put right
393 **slumbered:** slept
395 **idle:** trivial
395 **theme:** story
396 **No more yielding but:** means as little as
397 **Gentles:** ladies and gentlemen
397 **reprehend:** tell us off
398 **mend:** put it right
401 **'scape:** escape
401 **the serpent's tongue:** hissing from the audience
402 **make amends:** make it up to you
402 **ere:** before
405 **Give me your hands:** clap your hands
406 **restore amends:** make it up to you

109

EXAMINER'S NOTES, 5.1

These questions help you to explore many aspects of *A Midsummer Night's Dream.* Support each answer by reference to the text. At GCSE, your teacher will tell you which aspects are relevant to how your Shakespeare response will be assessed.

EXAMINER'S TIP

A good response

A good response may make links between details in a scene and details in a scene before or after. This can show either that Shakespeare is sustaining an aspect of plot or character (i.e. doing something to reinforce it) or developing an aspect of plot character (i.e. making it more varied or complex).

For example, Bottom's enthusiastic belief in his own skill as an entertainer was shown in Act 1 Scene 2, and now in Act 5 lines 320–323.

USING THE VIDEO

Exploring interpretation and performance

If you have looked at the video extracts in Dynamic Learning try this question.

The comedy in a performance sometimes depends entirely on the script, but sometimes it depends on what is added to the script.

Look at the part of the scene where Wall is on stage (lines 126–201). How does the performance create audience laughter by making the prop an active device on stage?

1 Character and plot development

This last Act is a single scene with the performance of the Mechanicals' play to the on-stage audience, the blessing of all marriages by Oberon and Titania, and Puck's Epilogue. It includes all the main characters of the play and after the confusions of the previous Acts, sets a mood of comic relaxation and happiness that all has ended well.

1 How does Shakespeare link Act 5 lines 1–41 with the action and mood of Act 1 Scene 1 and the events that follow?

2 What do you think the audience will be expecting from the Mechanicals' performance given that they saw the rehearsal in Act 3 Scene 1?

3 How does Shakespeare develop the character of Theseus in Act 5?

4 Why do you think Shakespeare chose Puck to deliver the Epilogue and how does it link with his role throughout the play?

2 Characterisation and voice: dramatic language

This scene is theatrically complex. Professional actors are playing roles as amateurs trying to be professionals. They skilfully show how unskilful bad actors can be. Shakespeare makes this easy by using common errors of reading and performing that he, as an actor, must have seen many times.

5 How does Shakespeare use the way people speak to create believable characters representing the lower classes in Athens (lines 108–117)?

6 How does Shakespeare use ideas and attitudes to create believable characters representing the upper classes in Athens (lines 118–125, 286–287)?

3 Themes and ideas

As a light-hearted comedy *A Midsummer Night's Dream* includes good-humoured exploration of fantasy; whether induced by love, drugs or dreams. Workmen imagine they are fine actors, the Queen of Fairies falls for an ass, and young lovers are in confusion. Weaving through the plots are aspects of life such as the nature of love, obedience, the supernatural, reality and imagination.

7 What ideas does Shakespeare present about the advantages and disadvantages of imagination in Theseus' speech (lines 212–219)?

8 Shakespeare uses the play within the play as a device to present theatrical performance as an illusion, similar to imagination, love, magic potions and dreams. What does he show about what these illusions have in common?

9 How does Shakespeare use Snug to show a character not quite sure of the difference between reality and fantasy in lines 213–220?

10 Shakespeare often uses last acts to wrap up the action with some sense of meaning or purpose. What meanings or messages might the audience take away from Puck's Epilogue on the nature of what they have seen as a 'vision' or 'but a dream' as they 'slumbered here'?

EXAMINER'S NOTES, 5.1

❹ Performance

This scene is one that actors and audiences enjoy because of its parody of bad writing and parody of bad acting. There is scope for exaggerated acting of the romantic and the tragic kind; for problems with props (Wall and Moonshine) and costume (Lion); and for comic casting of unsuitable workmen to the roles. As ever, the richest element is language – Shakespeare enjoys writing lines that mock bad writing, and show actors making a mess of the script. He must have had plenty of experience of both of these.

11 How would you advise the actors in the play within the play to make the most of the comic possibilities of Mechanicals playing for lords and ladies?

12 How would you advise the following actors to make their lines amusing?
- Peter Quince giving the Prologue (lines 108–150)
- Bottom as Pyramus (lines 167–178, 267, 281–282, 320–323)
- Snug as the Lion (lines 212–219 and 252)
- Flute as Thisbe (lines 302–317)

13 What would you advise a team of actors to do to make the on-stage audience interesting to the audience in the theatre?

❺ Contexts and responses

The play within the play creates a context which allows the theatre audience to respond not only to the Pyramus and Thisbe play, but also to the way the aristocrats react to it.

14 What do you think would be the different responses of people in the audience to the Mechanicals' play and the attitude of the stage audience?

15 If you were directing a film version, how would you present the play within the play, and the stage audience watching it?

16 What do you think would be more effective in the context of workmen playing for an aristocratic audience – to make the dance after line 331 elegant and delightful, or comically clumsy?

❻ Reflecting on the play

17 Which two short extracts from the play would you choose to explain Shakespeare's skill as a dramatist to someone who has never read or seen the play?

18 What do you think has made *A Midsummer Night's Dream* so popular in the theatre from Shakespeare's time to today?

19 In what ways has your enjoyment of the play been enhanced by performance on stage, on screen or in the classroom?

EXAMINER'S TIP

Writing about drama

The comedy based on the play within the play is an example of Shakespeare's skill in *literary parody*. He creates a badly-written play full of exaggerated speech effects such as repeated 'O!', exaggerated alliteration 'bloody breast', and predictable rhymes. He seems to enjoy making fun of the work of less talented writers.

Shakespeare also uses his knowledge of life in the theatre to create a *theatrical parody* of bad acting by uneducated amateurs, making comedy out of mispronunciation, poor punctuation, and slipping out of role. He may also be making a point about how rudely some upper class audiences might behave in the theatre.

EXAMINER'S TIP

Reflecting on the play

When writing about a character in a play, remember to comment on how he or she may show motives, feelings and reactions that are typical of ordinary people, or even ourselves. This helps to show appreciation of Shakespeare's skill in showing common human elements in characters on stage – and making us sometimes empathise with them as well as judge them.

1.1	Theseus, Duke of Athens, having defeated Hippolyta (Queen of the Amazons) in a war, plans to marry her. Egeus arrives with his daughter, Hermia, demanding she should marry Demetrius. She wants to marry Lysander. Theseus rules she must marry Demetrius or become a nun. Lysander and Hermia decide to run away, and tell Helena (Hermia's oldest friend, who is in love with Demetrius). Helena decides to tell Demetrius.
1.2	The Mechanicals (workmen from Athens) plan to put on a play to celebrate the wedding of Theseus and Hippolyta. Quince gives out the parts. They agree to meet in the wood the next night to rehearse.
2.1	Oberon and Titania (King and Queen of the Fairies) quarrel because Titania won't give him an Indian boy. Oberon plots to drug her so she falls in love with the next creature she sees. He wants to punish her, and to get her to give him the boy. Seeing Demetrius reject Helena, Oberon tells Puck to drug Demetrius to make him fall in love with her.
2.2	It is night. Titania sleeps. Oberon drops the love drug on her eyes. Hermia and Lysander enter, and decide to sleep. Puck sees Lysander, assumes he is Demetrius, and gives him the drug. Demetrius abandons Helena. She sees Lysander, and wakes him, fearing he might be dead. Lysander wakes and is besotted with Helena.
3.1	The Mechanicals meet in the woods to rehearse. Puck follows Bottom offstage and transforms him by giving him a donkey's head. When Bottom re-enters, the workmen are terrified and run away. Bottom sings, waking Titania, and the drug works again – she falls for him, and takes him off to her bed.
3.2	Puck tells Oberon about Titania and Bottom. Demetrius and Hermia enter. Oberon realises Puck has drugged the wrong man. Oberon sends Puck to fetch Helena, while he drugs Demetrius. Helena enters, followed by Lysander claiming he loves her. This wakes Demetrius who also says he loves Helena. Helena thinks they are mocking her. The two men quarrel about who deserves Helena. Hermia appears, pleased to find Lysander. He tells her he now loves Helena. Hermia blames Helena. The two men go off to fight, and Hermia chases Helena off the stage. Oberon sends Puck to fetch the lovers, make them sleep, and give Lysander an antidote. All four lovers are left sleeping on the stage.
4.1	Bottom and Titania fall asleep. Oberon gives Titania the antidote. She wakes, horrified to see she has been in love with Bottom with the donkey's head. Her quarrel with Oberon is over. Puck removes the donkey's head. Bottom remains asleep. The Fairies leave. Theseus, Hippolyta and Egeus enter, and wake the lovers. Shocked to see Hermia with Lysander, Egeus demands Theseus punish Lysander. However, Demetrius intervenes and says he no longer wants to marry Hermia, because he now loves Helena. Theseus decides the two pairs of lovers can marry at the same time as he and Hippolyta do. They all leave for Athens. Bottom wakes, convinced he has had a strange dream. He goes to find the other Mechanicals.
4.2	The Mechanicals are miserable, as they cannot put on the play without Bottom. He arrives, telling them to get ready, because their play has been chosen for the wedding celebrations.
5.1	On the evening after the wedding, the Mechanicals perform their play so badly that Theseus, Hippolyta and the lovers make fun of them. After the play some of the Mechanicals perform a dance, then the newlyweds go to bed. Oberon and Titania bless the marriages, and lead the Fairies in a dance. Puck ends the play asking the audience for applause.

How to write a good response to *A Midsummer Night's Dream* for GCSE English Literature

Whatever Controlled Assessment task you take will be based on some of the Assessment Objectives below. Your teacher will tell you which ones are relevant to how your Shakespeare response will be assessed.

If you are taking GCSE English or GCSE English Language, some of the examples for the GCSE English Literature Assessment Objectives may be of use when preparing for your response to *A Midsummer Night's Dream.* Your teacher will tell you which ones are relevant to how your Shakespeare response will be assessed.

AO	GCSE English Literature Assessment Objectives	Key word used for each AO, below
1	Respond to texts critically and imaginatively; select and evaluate relevant textual detail to illustrate and support interpretations.	**Response**
2	Explain how language, structure and form contribute to writers' presentation of ideas, themes and settings.	**Language**
3	Make comparisons and explain links between texts, evaluating writers' different ways of expressing meaning and achieving effects.	**Comparison/Links**
4	Relate texts to their social, cultural and historical contexts; explain how texts have been influential and significant to self and other readers in different contexts.	**Contexts**

❶ Response

If you are assessed on Response (AO1), you need to:

- understand what you have read and can prove that you understand
- show some judgement based on informed knowledge about plays, language and Shakespeare but also based on your own feelings, attitudes and preferences
- always support what you write with relevant reference or quotation.

How do you show you can do this?

Write a comment on what Egeus says, showing not just that you understand what he means, but using supporting detail of your quotation to develop your comment and include your own feelings and attitudes. For example, if responding to Act 1 Scene 1 line 27:

Rather than: *Egeus thinks that Lysander has used some witchcraft to make his daughter fall in love with him.*

Write something such as: *Shakespeare shows that Egeus cannot believe that his daughter would be disobedient to him and fall in love with Lysander on her own accord, by having Egeus explain that Hermia has been under some spell, and that Lysander used 'witchcraft'. This shows the audience his belief that Hermia would not fall in love with Lysander by choice, so Lysander must be a cunning trickster who is not to be trusted and not worthy of his daughter. I think lots of fathers might think in this way because they don't want to believe that their precious daughter could fall for someone they don't approve of.*

This response shows understanding, relevant quotation, personal feelings and attitudes and a judgement based on Shakespeare's purpose as a playwright.

Now try it yourself with the question: What are Egeus' feelings about all the gifts that Lysander has given Hermia in Act 1 Scene 1 lines 28–35?

Rather than: *Egeus' feelings about Lysander's gifts are that they are not true signs of love,* using one or two quotations, write a paragraph in response which develops the point with supporting textual detail.

EXAMINER'S TIP

Response

- Respond thoughtfully and sensitively to the text.
- Pick out short, relevant phrases or quotations from the play to back up your ideas.
- Explain and analyse the quotations.

② Language

If you are assessed on Language (AO2), you need to have a good understanding of the writer's craft, including Shakespeare's technical skill in:

- choice of language
- composition of a text in scenes
- making people and situations believable
- making themes and ideas interesting.

How do you show you can do this?

Write a comment which shows that Shakespeare has used particular words and images in a speech so as to have an impact on the audience. For example, in Act 1 Scene 1 lines 65–78:

Rather than: *Theseus uses words to show Hermia won't be happy as a nun.*

Write something such as: *Shakespeare uses language in Theseus' speech which emphasises the harshness of a nun's life. He explains that she must 'endure' the livery of a nun, making the clothes sound uncomfortable. He says that she will be 'mewed', meaning imprisoned in a 'shady' cloister, which makes it seem dark and cold. He describes her duties as chanting 'faint' hymns at night to the 'cold, fruitless moon' which sounds distant and unproductive. Theseus is trying to warn her of the consequences of going against her father's will.*

Now try it yourself with the question: How does Shakespeare show that Hermia is not afraid to defy her father and speak her mind to the Duke in Act 1 Scene 1 lines 58–64?

Rather than: *Hermia's language is honest and direct,* using one or two quotations, write a paragraph developing the comment with supporting textual detail and comment on Shakespeare's choice of words to have an effect on the audience.

③ Comparison/Links

If you are assessed on Comparisons/Links (AO3), you need to:

- see what is similar in texts (e.g. themes, settings, situations) and what is different in texts (e.g. authors' attitudes, values, style and appeal to readers)
- give your opinion of how well the writers have used their craft to create effects on readers/audiences.

How do you show you can do this?

Your comparison or links will depend on the linked text you are studying. The example shows a comparison/link with a text where a setting can be directly described, and *A Midsummer Night's Dream* where Shakespeare has to use characters to set the scene, through their dialogue.

If commenting on creating a sense of place and mood (Act 2 Scene 1 lines 248–256, for example), rather than: *In this text the scene can be set by the author building a description directly into the narrative and setting but in A Midsummer Night's Dream, Shakespeare has to let the characters set the scene through what they say.*

Write something such as: *In this text a description of a scene can be given directly. For example, 'The bank was a place of natural beauty, a bed of wild flowers'. In A Midsummer Night's Dream, Shakespeare has to create a sense of*

EXAMINER'S TIP

Language

- Write about why Shakespeare has chosen particular words or phrases to get his meaning across.
- Write about the theme(s) of the play.
- Write about the setting of the play/particular scene.

This response comments on choice of language and the focus of a scene in the play as a whole, with an explanation of how the detail interests an audience and shows insight into real life.

EXAMINER'S TIP

Comparison/Links

Think about what is similar and what is different about the texts and the way they are written.

This response shows effective choice of detail and explanation of how the device helps the dramatic action on stage, as well as sustaining one of the themes of the play, where nature is a setting where Titania is comfortable and which reflects her own sensuous qualities.

place and mood by what the characters say, such as when Oberon describes the place where Titania is sleeping: 'I know a bank where the wild thyme blows'. This is where dialogue fills in the detail of what's happening or what's happened off stage. The details of the colourful and fragrant plants create a sense of natural beauty, a place chosen by Titania because she is comfortable surrounded by flowers and scents.

Now try it yourself with the question: How does Shakespeare use the words of Titania to create setting and mood in Act 2 Scene 1 lines 81–117? How does this compare with how setting and mood is created in the linked text you are studying?

Rather than: *Titania uses negative description of the countryside so the audience can imagine it as an ugly and unhealthy place because of their jealousy and Shakespeare couldn't show this countryside on stage*, using one or two quotations, write a paragraph in response, showing how Shakespeare uses the details in Titania's speech to create setting and mood. Compare it with an example of how a sense of setting and mood is created in the linked text you are studying.

4 Contexts

If you are assessed on Contexts (AO4), you need to:

- understand something about the culture that is reflected in the text because of the time or place it was written, or an aspect of the author's experience
- think about and explain what it is in your own life and culture that makes you interested (or not interested) in the text you have studied
- consider a personal response in a context of attitudes, values and beliefs of your personal culture. The most important thing about 'social, cultural or historical texts' is 'What's changed?' and 'What's stayed the same?'

How do you show you can do this?

Rather than: *People in Shakespeare's day might have thought Egeus had a point in expecting Hermia to obey him.*

Write something such as: *People don't judge things from the same point of view. In Shakespeare's day the audience would have understood that Egeus had a father's lawful right about his daughter's marriage partner. Although Egeus' reaction is extreme, he believes his daughter has been 'bewitched' by Lysander, and that Demetrius is better connected. More importantly, Shakespeare wanted a dramatic situation, and found it by setting the play in the context of ancient Athens and its law. A modern audience would think punishments of death or becoming a nun are outrageous and cruel, and that daughters should choose their marriage partner. They might understand that Egeus had good intentions but think he should respect Hermia's point of view.*

Now try it yourself with the question: How might members of an audience react differently to the way Shakespeare presents Theseus' guidance to Hermia (lines 46–90)?

Rather than: *Shakespeare presents Theseus as backing up that Hermia must do what her father demands*, using one or two quotations, write a paragraph in response, showing that some people in an audience may think that Theseus guides Hermia wisely, while others might think Hermia is right to disagree and still refuse to marry Demetrius.

This response shows understanding of how attitudes and values can result in different interpretations and responses.

EXAMINER'S TIP

Contexts

Show that you understand how people in different audiences may respond differently based on their own background, attitudes and beliefs.

If you are writing about an audience in Shakespeare's time and today, show you understand how events or attitudes or customs at the time in which the play is set or the time in which the play was written may have had an influence on Shakespeare's writing.

Although you need to have an understanding of these issues, remember that the play itself is your main focus. Only mention details about the playwright or period if it is relevant to what you are discussing about the play.

These key terms provide a starting place for exploring key aspects of *A Midsummer Night's Dream*. At GCSE, your teacher will tell you which examples are most relevant to how your Shakespeare response will be assessed.

THEMES AND IDEAS

Appearance, illusion and deception v. reality

True love

Egeus wrongly accuses Lysander of 'feigning love' 1.1. 31 to bewitch Hermia to love him Egeus believes Demetrius is the appropriate choice for Hermia 1.1. 40–5 but he is reported as 'inconstant' 1.1. 110 and later reveals he was betrothed to Helena 4.1. 170–1

Playing a part

Bottom believes he is a fine actor and can play any part 1.2; he is then cast by a spell into another role as an ass without knowing it 3.1. 91–109 and when out of the spell remembers it as a 'rare vision' 4.1. 204
The Mechanicals describe the classical tragedy of the death of lovers, *Pyramus and Thisbe*, as a 'lamentable comedy' 1.2. 10 and the quality of their acting skills presents tragedy as comedy 5.1
The Mechanicals believe their performance is so convincing that the audience won't tell reality from appearance 3.1. 24–40 and they struggle to create illusions for the audience 3.1. 41–62

Supernatural influence/Transformation

Supernatural beings can change shape and be an unknown cause of mischief in the human world 2.1. 43–57
The love potion makes Lysander fall in love with Helena 2.2. 80–5, 107–126
Puck transforms Bottom so he has an ass' head and is unaware of the transformation 3.1. 91–109
The love potion makes Titania fall in love with Bottom as an ass 2.2. 31–8; 3.1. 122–143; 4.1. 1–44
The love potion makes Demetrius fall in love with Helena 3.2. 105, 137–144
Lysander and Demetrius, affected by the love potion, both love Helena and fight over her 3.2. 137–405
Puck and Oberon watch the 'pageant' they have created for the 'fools these mortals be' 3.2. 114–5
Helena and Hermia fight because Helena thinks Demetrius and Lysander are pretending to love her and it's a trick 3.2. 145–161, 192–344
Puck gives Lysander an antidote to the love potion 3.2. 449–464 so his love returns to Hermia 4.1. 145–199
Oberon gives an antidote to the love potion to Titania and her love returns to him 4.1. 69–82
Puck restores Bottom 4.1. 83 so he is no longer an ass and thinks he has had a 'rare vision' 4.1. 204–14
Waking lovers remain confused as to what is real and what was a dream 4.1. 140–199

Conflict

Between male and female

Theseus v Hippolyta 1.1. 16–17; Oberon and Titania's jealousy disrupts both fairy world 2.1. 18–31 and human world 2.1. 81–117

Unrequited/Disappointed love

Hermia scorns Demetrius 1.1. 46–82; Demetrius scorns Helena 2.1. 188–244, Lysander scorns Hermia 3.2 186–190; confusion between the lovers 3.2. 220–44

Between rivals

Lysander and Demetrius declare love for Hermia 1.1. 91–4 then for Helena 3.2. 169–176, 248–255

In family relationships

Egeus believes a daughter should obey her father 1.1. 23–90; the father's right to choose the daughter's husband is enshrined in Athenian law 1.1. 41–4; the Duke can override a father's rights 4.1. 176–180

Between friends

Helena and Hermia 3.2. 192–344

Resolution of conflict

Wedding plans for Theseus and Hippolyta 1.1. 18–19
Lysander is released from the love potion 3.2. 450 and restored to Hermia 4.1. 145–199
Titania is restored to Oberon 4.1. 69–82
Theseus releases Hermia to marry Lysander and allows Demetrius, still under the influence of the love potion, to marry Helena 4.1. 176–180

Dreams and sleep

The love potion is administered when asleep to:
Titania 2.2. 30–8 who then loves ass-headed Bottom 3.1. 114–180, 4.1. 1–144
Lysander 2.2. 74–87 who then loves Helena 2.2. 106–126; Demetrius 3.2. 88–109 who then loves Helena 3.2. 137–173
Hermia wakes from a nightmare to discover that Lysander is gone 2.2. 149–160 and that he now loves Helena 3.2. 271–281
The magic is released when asleep for:
Titania 4.1. 69–74 who thinks she has seen 'visions' 4.1. 75 and her love for Oberon is restored; Bottom 4.1. 83 who thinks he has had a 'rare vision' and returns to the Mechanicals 4.1. 200–214; Lysander 3.2. 449–464 whose love is restored to Hermia 4.1. 145–152

Sleep ends and the lovers' problems are overcome; Demetrius remains in love with Helena; waking lovers remain confused as to what is real and what was a dream 4.1. 140–199
Theseus' view is that imagination causes lovers, madmen and poets to dream strange things 5.1. 2–22
Puck suggests the whole play might be a vision or the audience's dream 5.1. 391–6

Identity and status

Skilled actors act as unskilled actors (the Mechanicals) trying to be skilled actors 1.2, 3.1. 1–105, 4.2, 5.1. 108–330
The Mechanicals take on other identities in their play and Bottom is willing to take on all of them 1.2
Bottom changes identity and status from a Mechanical to an ass who is loved by the Queen of Fairies and is waited on by fairy servants 3.1. 91–180; 4.1. 1–44 then is returned to the Mechanicals 4.1. 83; 200–214
Titania changes identity and status from Oberon's lover and Queen of the Fairies to being besotted with ass-headed Bottom 3.1. 122–180; 4.1. 1–44 and back to Oberon's lover and Queen 4.1. 69–74
Puck mistakes identity and administers the love potion to Lysander thinking he is Demetrius 2.2. 76–85
Lysander and Demetrius both lose their identity as Hermia's lovers and become Helena's lovers 3.2. 169–172, 249–253; Lysander is restored to Hermia 3.2. 449–464, 4.1. 145–152 though Demetrius remains in love with Helena 4.1. 159–199
Helena and Hermia lose their identity as friends 3.2. 192–244 and are joined again in the confusion of what is real or a dream 4.1. 176–199
The play within the play contrasts the Mechanicals' lower identity and status both in and out of roles, with the higher status of the on-stage audience and their comments 5.1
The identity and status of the audience is considered in Puck's Epilogue, as audience of the play or part of the dream 5.1. 391–396

Love and marriage

Theseus and Hippolyta come through war to marriage 1.1. 16–19
Titania and Oberon, Queen and King of the fairies, quarrel because each wants the 'changeling boy' 2.1. 18–27 and are jealous of each other's interest in humans 2.1. 64–80; their power struggle causes disorder in the supernatural world 2.1. 18–31 and the natural world 2.1. 81–117; Oberon uses the love potion to make Titania fall in love with ass-headed Bottom 2.2. 31–8; 3.1. 122–143; Oberon then restores Titania and her love returns to him 4.1. 69–82
In the play within the play of *Pyramus and Thisbe* the lovers are thwarted by parental disapproval, and when trying to meet secretly, Pyramus believes the lion killed Thisbe with tragic outcomes 5.1. 275–286

The young lovers before the love potion

'The course of true love never did run smooth' for Lysander and Hermia 1.1. 134; before marriage can be achieved, true love overcomes obstacles; e.g. Egeus' choice of Demetrius for Hermia 1.1. 40, the use of Athenian law to try and make Hermia obey him 1.1. 41–5 Hermia's plea to Theseus 1.1. 58–64; the plan to run away to marry 1.1. 156–178
Helena's unrequited love for Demetrius results in jealousy 1.1. 180–225 so Helena betrays Hermia's plans, hoping to win back Demetrius 1.1. 226–252, 2.1. 238–242 but Demetrius scorns Helena's humble and fawning love 2.1. 202–213

The young lovers influenced by the love potion

Puck and Oberon comment on 'what fools these mortals be' 3.2. 114–15 as they watch the 'pageant' unfold as Lysander falls in love with Helena 2.2. 80–5, 107–126; Demetrius falls in love with Helena and love changes how he values her 1.1. 232–5, 3.2. 105–7, 137–173; Lysander and Demetrius become jealous rivals over Helena 3.2. 137–405; Helena scorns both lovers because she thinks they are just pretending to love her 3.2. 283; Lysander scorns Hermia 3.2. 260–1
Helena and Hermia fight because Helena thinks Demetrius and Lysander are pretending to love her and it's a trick 3.2. 145–161, 192–344

Young love resolved

Puck gives Lysander an antidote to the love potion 3.2. 449–464 and his love returns to Hermia
Demetrius remains in love with Helena and admits to Egeus his previous betrothal to Helena 4.1. 159–175
Theseus overrules Egeus and decides that all three marriages will take place on the same day: Theseus and Hippolyta, Lysander and Hermia, Demetrius and Helena 4.1. 176–180
Waking lovers remain confused as to what is real and what was a dream 4.1. 186–199

Natural and supernatural

Properties of the supernatural world

Oberon and Titania are King and Queen of the fairy world, where spells are used to achieve their goals and they can steal children, change shape, create mischief 2.1. 1–58

Relationship between the supernatural and natural world

Fairies are often named after flowers (Peaseblossom) and natural objects (Cobweb) 3.1, sometimes worshipped by humans 2.1. 123; can love humans 2.1. 63–78

Effect on the natural world of the disharmony of the supernatural world

Oberon and Titania's jealousy causes a rift in their marriage bringing disharmony to: the fairy kingdom 2.1. 18–31; the natural world, weather and seasons 2.1. 64–117

Effect of the supernatural world's influence

The human world becomes confused and imbalanced 2.1. 32–57, 81–117
The magic potion given to sleeping lovers disrupt relationships with mischievous Puck's mistake in giving the love potion to Lysander 2.2. 81, Oberon correcting this by giving the love potion to Demetrius 3.2. 88–109, and them both enjoying the resulting 'pageant' 3.2. 110–121
Similarly, magic brings confusion and imbalance to the fairy world when Oberon gives the love potion to Titania 2.2. 31–8 making the fairy Queen fall in love with ass–headed working–class Bottom and the fairies serve him 3.1. 122–143; 4.1.1–44

Contrast of supernatural events of the wood with the order of Theseus' court

Athenian marriage law is clear that daughters should obey fathers 1.1. 47–51
Duke Theseus passes judgement 1.1. 84–90

Harmony of natural and supernatural world

The lovers' tensions are resolved as Lysander is released from the love potion 3.2. 450 and restored to Hermia 4.1. 145–199;
Titania is restored to Oberon 4.1. 69–82;
Theseus releases Hermia to marry Lysander and allows Demetrius, still under the influence of the love potion, to marry Helena, with the weddings held together with Theseus and Hippolyta 4.1. 176–180
Oberon, Titania, Puck and the fairies bless the marriages and offer protection 5.1. 370–390

CHARACTERISATION AND VOICE

Characterisation

The skill of making an actor playing a part do it so well that the audience believes he is a real person, with a distinct personality, attitudes, feelings and behaviour.
Characterisation can be developed by reported details, e.g. of Puck 2.1. 32–42 or by revealed behaviour, e.g. Bottom in 1.2

Voice

See examiner's tip p18
On stage, characters are created through the following:
Actor's use of voice: e.g. ways of speaking indicate status 1.1, mood 3.2. 289–299, thought processes and relationship in dialogue 1.1. 194–207
Public voices (indicating a character's high status): language can be formal, poetic and elaborate; e.g. 1.1. 1–15
Private voices (revealing feelings): vocabulary choices can be simpler, more active and direct; e.g. 1.1. 128–140
Speech habits: e.g. Bottom gets names and identities wrong, calling Hercules the Greek Hero a 'tyrant' named Ercles 1.2. 22–4; Thisbe becomes Thisne 1.2. 45; Ninus becomes 'Ninny' 3.1. 85
Fairies speak in short lines, often rhyming, especially when singing 2.1. 1–59, 2.2. 9–28 or casting a spell 2.2. 31–8, 2.2. 70–87
Fairy speech often includes flower imagery and nature 2.1. 82–114, 2.1. 248–256, 2.2. 19–22

LANGUAGE

Alliteration

Repetition of consonant sounds, especially at the beginning of words used to create:
Pace: 'thorough bush, thorough brier,/over park, over pale,/thorough flood, thorough fire' 2.1. 2–5; a sensual description of Titania's bed, 'lulled in these flowers with dances and delight./And there the snake throws her enamelled skin,/Weed wide enough to wrap a fairy in' 2.1. 254–6

Humour: 'bully Bottom' 3.1. 7, 'Whereat, with blade, with bloody blameful blade,/he bravely broached his boiling bloody breast' 5.1. 145–6

Allusions

Indirect references to other texts, especially the classics and mythology: e.g. Duke Theseus is a hero in Greek mythology who loved and abandoned many women before marrying Hippolyta 2.1. 76–80
Gods from Roman myths represent emotions e.g. Cupid (desire) and Venus (love) 1.1. 169–178, 2.1. 55–174
The myth of Pyramus and Thisbe's thwarted and tragic love is echoed in some events of the play e.g. parent forbids lovers to wed 1.1. 38–45; lovers arrange to meet secretly at night 1.1. 156–168; confusion separates them 2.2. 39–42, 82–7, 107–126, 149–160

Antithesis

The use of opposites and contrast: e.g.
The amateur performance of *Pyramus and Thisbe* 1.2, 3.1. 1–105, 4.2, 5.1. 108–330 contrasts with the professional *A Midsummer Night's Dream*
Within speeches: e.g. antithesis creates humour in Puck's mischief 2.1. 43–57; expresses longing in Helena's unrequited love for Demetrius and the contrasting effect of Hermia 1.1. 181–201; shows the impact of forbidden love on Hermia 1.1. 128–9; expresses conflict between characters 2.1. 212–3
Characters are contrasted e.g. Helena and Hermia 2.2. 117–8

Assonance

Repetition of vowel sounds to make a line sound longer or more emotional e.g. 'But O, methinks, how slow/This old moon wanes!' 1.1. 3–4

Hyperbole

Exaggeration used to emphasise a point e.g. Demetrius admires Helena 'To what, my love, shall I compare thine eyne?/Crystal is muddy' 3.2. 137–144

Imagery

Language chosen to put vivid, usually visual images in the audience's head e.g.:

Eyes

Hermia wishes Egeus saw Lysander with her eyes 1.1. 56; Theseus retorts she should look with her father's judgement 1.1. 57; eyes attract love 2.2. 95–6 and love is conveyed through lover's eyes 2.2. 125–6, 131

Flowers and fruit

Cowslips are bodyguards in the fairy world 2.1.10–15; flowers form Titania's bed 2.1. 249–254; since love-in-idlesess was struck by Cupid's bow its juice makes people fall in love 2.1. 165–172; roses symbolise sexual love 1.1. 76–8, Titania sticks roses in Bottom's ass' head 4.1.3, after Theseus' ruling Lysander notices Hermia's cheek 'roses' are fading fast 1.1. 128–9, Oberon and Titania's row brings frost to the 'lap' of fresh roses 2.1. 107–8; paired cherries symbolise Helena and Hermia's friendship 3.2. 209–11

Blood
Symbolises desire, and differences in desire that inhibit love 1.1. 135; death 2.2. 105, 3.2. 48, 3.2. 75, 5.1. 142, 5.1. 268

Nature
Animals are used in spells; e.g. snakes, newts 2.2. 9–22; as metaphor; e.g. serpent 2.2. 149–152; for humour; e.g. lion; 3.1. 26–40; Puck's animal forms 3.1. 97–100; Helena as a spaniel 2.1. 203–10, as a bear 2.2. 98; Bottom translated to an ass 3.1. 90–107; animals used in insults: dog, cur, snake 3.2. 65–73, serpent 260–1

Moon
Measures time; e.g. until Hippolyta and Theseus' wedding 1.1. 1–11; moonlight aided Lysander as he supposedly feigned love, singing at Hermia's window 1.1. 30–1; the fruitless moon symbolises chastity if Hermia's disobedience means she becomes a nun 1.1. 70–3; the new moon is the deadline for Hermia's decision 1.1. 83; moonlight is the time for: fairies' activity 2.1. 60, 141, Pyramus and Thisbe's meeting 3.1. 43, Cupid's flights 2.1. 161–4; the Mechanicals' character Moonshine adds humour 5.1. 229–250

Irony

Dramatic irony
Leads to humour and conflict: e.g. Puck does not know he is putting juice in the wrong Athenian's eye 2.2. 76–85; unaware of the magic, Helena believes Lysander and Demetrius make fun of her when they declare their love 3.2. 137–342

Verbal irony
Bottom never discovers he was transformed with the head of an ass, leading to verbal irony; e.g. 3.1. 104, 106, 4.1. 22–6, 31–3
Demetrius' comment on asses' speaking 5.1. 152

Situational irony
Demetrius and Lysander both love Hermia, not Helena 1.1, then Helena not Hermia 3.2; Demetrius scorning Helena's love 2.1, then Helena scorning Demetrius' love 3.2

Onomatopoeia
Where sounds of words echo their sense: e.g. Puck's changing form 'neighing' in likeness of a filly foal 2.1. 46; Titania and Oberon's jealousy affects the weather with e.g. 'whistling' wind 2.1. 86 and contagious fogs 'sucked' up from the sea 2.1. 89

Oxymorons
Phrases made up of opposites: e.g.: 'make a heaven of hell' emphasises the strength of Helena's emotions for Demetrius 2.1. 243; adds to humour: the Mechanicals' play is 'merry and tragical', 'tedious and brief' and 'hot ice and wondrous strange snow' 5.1. 56–60

Parody
Imitation of a characteristic style of an author or work for comic effect: the parody of melodramatic writing for the Mechanicals e.g. Bottom as Pyramus 'O grim–looked night… O night, alack, alack' 5.1. 167–178; and for the lovers; e.g. Hermia, 'O me, what news, my love?' 'O me! … You thief of love!' 3.2 271–284
The tragedy of Pyramus and Thisbe is used humorously to parody events with the secret plans of the lovers in the play 1.1. 156–178, 5.1. 135–7
Peter Quince's Prologue 5.1. 108–17 parodies Puck's epilogue 5.1. 391–406
Pyramus and Thisbe's speeches parody lovers' compliments e.g. 3.2. 137–144, 5.1.302–17
Use of alliteration in verse is humorously parodied 5.1. 146–7

Personification
Words used to put human or animal characteristics onto non–human or non–animal things; e.g. love 'looks' 1.1. 234; frowns 'teach' 1.1.195; Wall and Moonlight are personified in the Mechanicals' play 3.1. 58–61 adding humour 5.1. 229–250

Verse and prose

Blank verse
Used for much of the play: a regular pattern of emphasis that is not written in rhyme but helps the actor speak the lines; e.g.: 'Four **days** will **quick**ly **steep** them**selves** in **night**,/Four **nights** will **quick**ly **dream** a**way** the **time**' 1.1. 7–8

Prose language
Everyday speech often used by characters of lower social status such as the Mechanicals; e.g. 'You were best to call them generally, man by man, /according to the scrip' 1.2. 2–3

Rhyming poetry
Often used for speeches of the lovers and fairies; e.g. 'I know a bank where the wild thyme blows,/Where oxlips and the nodding violet grows' 2.1. 249–250

Iambic pentameter
A pattern of five pairs of unstressed then stressed syllables in a line; e.g. 'The **course** of **true** love **nev**er **did** run **smooth**' 1.1. 134 and shared lines where different characters complete an iambic pentameter to increase the pace; e.g. 3.1. 146

Word play
Adds humour, entertainment and ambiguous meanings: e.g. double meanings: hail 1.1. 243–5; 'wood' means both trees and in a fury 2.1. 191–2, lie 2.2. 56–61
Malapropisms: 'aggravate' instead of 'moderate' 1.2. 71, 'odious savours sweet' instead of 'odours savours sweet' 3.1. 72–3, 'Ninny' instead of 'Ninus' 3.1. 85–6 Creates irony 3.1. 106
Bottom's jokes about fairies' names 3.1. 161–175
Punctuation misplaced 5.1. 108–125

PERFORMANCE: STAGECRAFT AND THEATRICALITY

Soliloquies
Audience engagement and character revelation of feelings and insights: e.g. Helena reveals her reasons for betraying Hermia's plans 1.1. 226–251; Oberon reveals his plan for Titania 2.1. 176–87; Puck shows the audience his misunderstanding 2.2. 70–87; Hermia evokes pity and suspense as she wakes alone, not knowing what the audience knows about Lysander and Helena 2.2. 149–160

Stage directions
Enabling actors to make the most of performance: e.g.:
Stage directions for action such as giving the flower juice 2.1. 259; reading a book 3.1. 47; Bottom entering in an ass's head 3.1. 92
Embedded directions in the text acting as cues for actors; e.g. Puck to girdle the earth 2.1. 175–6; Oberon making himself invisible to overhear Demetrius 2.1. 186–7

Structure
The way a play is built with different parts doing different jobs to maintain interest and exploit contrasts, such as setting the scene, and introducing or developing a character or plot. In this play plot parallels and contrasts are used to create dramatic structure, e.g. Theseus and Hippolyta will rule Athens 1.1; Oberon and Titania the fairy kingdom 2.1
The play within the play of the tragedy of the forbidden lovers Pyramus and Thisbe 5.1 contrasts with the union of the forbidden lovers Hermia and Lysander 4.1. 176–180
The humorous bad acting of the play within the play by the Mechanicals is commented on by the stage audience 5.1
The confusions, contrasts and strands within the play are resolved and brought together with the weddings of the three pairs of lovers, the Mechanicals' play, and the blessing of the fairies 5.1
Puck suggests the whole play might be a vision or the audience's dream 5.1. 391–396

Settings
The ordered reasoning of the palace 1.1 contrasts with the dreamlike imagination of the wood 2.1 forward; in the daytime human law, order and reality rule 1.1 contrasting with the night when fairy power, confusion and illusions abound 2.2.39 onwards

Characters
For example, tall Helena contrasts with short Hermia creating comedy 3.2. 289–298; beautiful Titania is made to fall in love with ass-headed Bottom 3.1 114–144, 4.1. 1–44; clumsy, prose speaking Mechanicals' world e.g. 1.2 versus graceful verse-speaking fairy world; e.g. 2.1;

Mechanicals known by their occupation; e.g. Nick Bottom the weaver 1.2. 15; fairies known by plant names; e.g. Peaseblossom, Cobweb 4.1

Theatricality
Bottom's ass' head 3.1. 91; lovers' tiffs 3.2. 45 onwards; magic spells on Titania 2.2. 31–8, Lysander 2.2. 82–7, Demetrius 3.2. 103–9, waking Lysander 3.2. 450–464, waking Titania 4.1. 70–4; songs e.g. 2.2. 9 and dances e.g. 4.1. 83–91; 5.1. 365–390

Actor's view
Bottom (Paul Hunter, 2008) 20
Demetrius (Richard James–Neale, 2012) 58
A Fairy (and Helena) (Carlyss Peer, 2012) 38
Flute/Thisbe (Peter Bray, 2012) 88
Giles Block (Shakespeare's Globe text consultant) 38
Hermia (Louise Collins, 2012) 12, 40, 56, 66, 84
Hippolyta and Titania (Siobhan Redmond, 2008) 8, 26
Hippolyta (Emma Pallant, 2012) 90
Lysander (Peter Bray 2012) 40, 42, 64
Oberon (Chook Sibtain, 2012) 26
Puck (Fergal McElherron, 2012) 75
Snug/Lion (Louise Collins, 2012) 100

CONTEXTS

Contexts within the play that create a scene or mood
The palace is associated with formality and law keeping: 1.1, 4.1, 5.1; the woods are associated with fairy magic and freedom from conventions – which can be disturbing and unexpected; e.g. 2.1. 214–246

Context around the play
For example, the way that ideas, customs and events of the period are reflected in the play. See *Shakespeare's World*
Hippolyta and Theseus 6
Arranged marriages 8
Mechanicals performing plays 20
Boys and men playing women 22
Cue scripts 24
Fairies 24
Robin Goodfellow/Puck 26
A changeling 28
Weather lore 28
The tiring house 44
Props and scenery 46
Stage directions in the text 46
'You speak all your part at once, cues and all' 48

Clowns, Will Kemp, and Bottom 76
Betrothal 82
Cuts to the text 90
Performing at the royal court 94
Dumb shows 94
Who was Shakespeare making fun of? 100

Context of performance
Where and how the play is performed and how that affects the audience's understanding – e.g. characters in modern costume or Elizabethan dress

Globe Education Shakespeare

Series Editors: Fiona Banks, Paul Shuter, Patrick Spottiswoode

Steering Committee: Fiona Banks, Hayley Bartley, Paul Shuter, Patrick Spottiswoode, Shirley Wakley

A Midsummer Night's Dream

Editors: Fiona Banks, Paul Shuter

Consultant: Shirley Wakley

Play text: Hayley Bartley, Hilary Crain, Paul Shuter, Patrick Spottiswoode

Glossary: Jane Shuter

Assessment: Senior moderators and senior examiners including Peter Thomas, Paula Adair, Tony Farrell; key terms index: Clare Constant

From the rehearsal room: Fiona Banks, Georghia Ellinas, Yolanda Vazquez

Shakespeare's World Farah Karim-Cooper, Gwilym Jones, Amy Kenny, Paul Shuter, Simon Smith

Dynamic Learning: Hayley Batley

Progression: Georghia Ellinas, Michael Jones

Globe Education would like to thank our dedicated team of Globe Education Practitioners – who daily bring rehearsal room practices into the classroom for young people at Shakespeare's Globe and around the world. Their work is the inspiration for this series.

Photo credits

All photographs are from the Shakespeare's Globe Photo library.
Pete le May: 2; John Tramper: 3.
Donald Cooper, 2002 production, 8, 14C, 24C, 46B, 48A, 50A, 58B, 96B,
Manuel Harlan, 2008 production, 12, 14A, 16, 20, 22C, 24A, 28, 30, 32, 44A, 46A, 48B, 50B, 56, 58A, 62, 64, 68, 70A, 72, 76, 80, 84, 88, 92, 94, 96A, 100, 102B, 104B, 106
Ellie Kurttz, 2012 production, 6, 10, 14B, 22A, 22B, 26, 34, 38, 40, 42, 44B, 48C, 50C, 52, 54, 66, 70B, 74, 78, 82, 90, 98, 102A, 104A, 108.

Every effort has been made to trace all copyright holders, but if any have been inadvertently overlooked the Publishers will be pleased to make the necessary arrangements at the earliest opportunity.

Orders: please contact Bookpoint Ltd, 130 Milton Park, Abingdon, Oxon OX14 4SB. Telephone: (44) 01235 827720. Fax: (44) 01235 400454. Lines are open 9.00 – 5.00, Monday to Saturday, with a 24-hour message answering service. Visit our website at www.hoddereducation.co.uk

Cover photo © Donald Cooper
Illustrations by DC Graphic Design Limited, Swanley Village, Kent
Typeset in Garth Graphic Regular 10pt by DC Graphic Design Limited, Swanley Village, Kent
Printed in Dubai

A catalogue record for this title is available from the British Library

ISBN: 978 1444 136 66 1

Playing Shakespeare with Deutsche Bank

The 2012 production of *A Midsummer Night's Dream*, which features in this book, was the 2012 Playing Shakespeare with Deutsche Bank production. This is Globe Education's flagship programme for London schools, with 16,000 free tickets given to students for a full-scale Shakespeare production created specifically for young people.

www.playingshakespeare.org